PUSH A BUTTON

and be a submarine captain, a fighter pilot, a big-time gambler, a hunter or a prophet! Have a contest with your friends, competing on calculators. You have number knowledge in the palm of your hand, fun at your fingertips with your pocket calculator.

You don't have to be a mathwhiz to be a GAMES mastermind. You will find, though, that after you've played a number of the games in this book, you'll be handling the math in your school, business or daily life with greater ease.

SPECIAL FOR THE CALCU-COLLECTOR!

Included is a section with photographs and descriptions of some of the more unusual calculators on the market.

Books by Wallace Judd

Dogfight and More Games Calculators Play

Games Calculators Play

Published by
WARNER BOOKS

DOGFIGHT

& MORE GAMES CALCULATORS PLAY

BY WALLACE JUDD

WARNER BOOKS

A Warner Communications Company

This book is dedicated to all the students in my calculator class at Walter Hays School in Palo Alto. Their interest and constant enthusiasm inspired many of these new games. And their ability to find and exploit ambiguities in the directions resulted in many refinements in the original rules.

WARNER BOOKS EDITION

Variations of the games, "The Big One," "Bullseye," "Nim," "After," "Before" and "Wipeout", previously appeared in an article by the author for ARITHMETIC TEACHER, Nov. 1976, Vol. 23, No. 7, and are adapted with permission.

The cartoon on page 70 is by Bill Eral. The photograph of the overhead demonstration calculator on page 73 was taken with the help of David Rubin and Susan Dutcher. The photograph of the chip on page 98 is by John Dexter. Telesensory Systems supplied the photograph of the Speech-Plus **TM** Calculator. All other photographs are by the author.

ISBN 0-446-84398-9

Cover design by The New Studio Inc.
Text design, artwork and typography by Arthur Ritter, Inc.

Warner Books, Inc., 75 Rockefeller Plaza, New York, N.Y. 10019

 A Warner Communications Company

Printed in the United States of America

Not associated with Warner Press, Inc. of Anderson, Indiana

First Printing: September, 1977

10 9 8 7 6 5 4 3 2 1

CONTENTS

Games of Chance

Kiddie Corner

Pattern Play

INTRODUCTION

The games in this book are for people who like to have fun with calculators and who enjoy sharing the fun with others.

For most of the games, the calculator serves, in lieu of a deck of cards or a set of dice, to create a chance situation in which a player finds himself pitted against the skill and luck of one or more opponents.

None of the games requires a complicated calculator—they can all be played on any simple, garden-variety four-function unit. And with so many low-cost calculators on the market today, assembling a calculator apiece for three, four or more players is no great task.

For most of the games that have some sort of board or chart, it is a good idea for the players to copy the chart in an enlarged version to play on. Keeping this size book folded open is quite a task, and the dimensions of the page make it hard to place the markers accurately on the game board. Where markers are necessary, it's a good idea to get some of the little plastic animals found at variety stores. They're colorful and serve as stable, easily-identifiable markers—and they only cost about a quarter apiece.

In the Solutions section you will find not only the answers to the puzzle and maze problems in the section *Games for One Person,* but also hints and strategies for playing some of the more complex games. So if you're playing a game and would like to make more sophisticated moves, see if the Solutions section can't give you some tips.

You will notice in the text that numbers with four or more digits do not have commas, just as calculators do not have commas. This avoids the possibility of mistaking a comma for a decimal point. Long numbers in most instances are printed with spaces every three digits to help you read them. For example, the number 4093847, is written 4 093 847, so it is obvious at a glance that it's seven digits long. Long decimals are treated in the same way. The number .000 007 is substantially easier to read and key in than .000007. For the latter, one practically needs to point at each of the zeros while counting them.

Here's to happy days of reckoning—figuratively, that is.

GAMES OF SKILL

The games in this section are all ones that give the players a chance to pit their skill against each other. In most of these games, there is a slight chance factor, as in the event of an initial lucky guess or an intuitive trial. But the single most important factor in winning is a familiarity with the number system and an ability to estimate quickly and accurately.

The directions don't specify time limits because most players don't need them—but if you find play moving too slowly, setting a time limit of, say, 15 or 30 seconds on each player's move should put some zip into the proceedings and make the game that much more exciting.

The games themselves are comparatively short. Most take no longer than five minutes to play. And you'll find them even more fun after you've played them a few times, because both you and your opponent will be trying to figure out a strategy to outfox each other.

Dogfight

Involves: Two players and two calculators.

Object: To "shoot down" the other player by getting his number on your calculator.

How to play: Each player covertly enters a number from 20 to 99 on his calculator. The number may *not* end in zero.

The numbers picked are then revealed, and each player in turn multiplies or divides the number on his display by any number as he tries to match the number on his opponent's display.

If a player goes over 100, the first digit is dropped. In other words, a player who unintentionally arrives at, say, 156, should reset his display to read 56 instead.

If an answer comes up with a decimal part, it is rounded off to the nearest whole number. (Some calculators have a switch that reads F 0 2 and will round off automatically when the switch is put at 0.)

The first player to get to the number on his opponent's display is the winner.

Sample Game

John and Peter each secretly key a number (from 20 to 99) into their calculators. Then they both show their displays. John's reads 49, Peter's shows 71. Peter lets John go first. Play proceeds as follows:

> John keys
> $49 \times 1.7 = 83.3$
> (rounded to 83)

> Peter tries to get to 83:
> $71 \times 1.2 = 85.2$
> (rounded to 85)

John, only two away
from Peter, tries to
get to 85.
83 x 1.06 = 87.98
(rounded to 88)

Peter tries something
tricky.
85 ÷ .8 = 106.25
   goes to 6
(Since Peter has gone over
100, the 1 is dropped,
putting him at 6, instead
of 106.)

John has to drop fast.
88 ÷ 11.3 = 7.787 610 6
(rounded to 8)

Peter sees his opening.
6 x 1.3 = 7.8
(rounded to 8)

Peter has matched the number on John's display, so
Peter wins.

Variations

Easier: Keep the starting numbers between one and ten.
This is suitable for early-grade elementary school children.

Harder: Allow the players to go from one to a thousand.
In this version, all players start at numbers bigger than 101,
and any total that comes up over 1000 loses the first digit.
Thus, if a player got to, say, 1017 he would change it to 17,
eliminating the zero as well.

The Spider and the Fly

Involves: Two players and two calculators.

Plus: An enlarged copy of the garden layout, as shown on facing page; pencil, ruler, and a small marker to represent the fly.

Object: For the spider to spin a web and trap the fly in 15 moves or less.

How to play: The spider and the fly both move around the garden in the same way—they multiply or divide the number on their calculators by any number they choose that suits their strategy. Each answer (rounded) determines their next position. For example, if the spider is at 42 and multiplies by 1.38, he gets 57.96, so he moves to 58. Any time the spider moves, he makes an X where he lands, and draws a line (his "web") from the X to the place he was last.

The fly can move anywhere, except he can't cross or touch the web. If he tries to make a move that would take him across the web, he loses his turn and doesn't get to move at all.

The fly starts first. The spider and the fly take turns until the fly can't move. The spider has to trap the fly in 15 moves or less.

Note: If the spider lands on or goes directly through the same spot as the fly, the fly gets to move to any spot in the garden—regardless of the web.

THE GARDEN

FLY STARTS HERE

1	2	3	4	5	6	7	8	9	10
11	12	13	14	15	16	17	18	19	20
21	22	23	24	25	26	27	28	29	30
31	32	33	34	35	36	37	38	39	40
41	42	43	44	45	46	47	48	49	50
51	52	53	54	55	56	57	58	59	60
61	62	63	64	65	66	67	68	69	70
71	72	73	74	75	76	77	78	79	80
81	82	83	84	85	86	87	88	89	90
91	92	93	94	95	96	97	98	99	100

SPIDER STARTS HERE

Fetch a "fly": All you need here is a small marker to "fly" around the garden.

Sample Game

Fly moves out of corner (10 x 6.7 = 67) and lands on 67. Spider (91 ÷ 3.5 = 26) moves to 26.

(Continued)

13

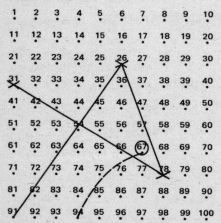

```
  1   2   3   4   5   6   7   8   9  10
 11  12  13  14  15  16  17  18  19  20
 21  22  23  24  25  26  27  28  29  30
 31  32  33  34  35  36  37  38  39  40
 41  42  43  44  45  46  47  48  49  50
 51  52  53  54  55  56  57  58  59  60
 61  62  63  64  65  66  67  68  69  70
 71  72  73  74  75  76  77  78  79  80
 81  82  83  84  85  86  87  88  89  90
 91  92  93  94  95  96  97  98  99 100
```

The fly moves away, and the spider tries to close off part of the garden. Fly (67 x 1.4 = 93.8) goes to 94. Spider (26 x 3 = 78) moves to 78.

```
  1   2   3   4   5   6   7   8   9  10
 11  12  13  14  15  16  17  18  19  20
 21  22  23  24  25  26  27  28  29  30
 31  32  33  34  35  36  37  38  39  40
 41  42  43  44  45  46  47  48  49  50
 51  52  53  54  55  56  57  58  59  60
 61  62  63  64  65  66  67  68  69  70
 71  72  73  74  75  76  77  78  79  80
 81  82  83  84  85  86  87  88  89  90
 91  92  93  94  95  96  97  98  99 100
```

Fly tries to get to 79, but misses (94 ÷ 1.4 = 67.142 857) and lands on 67. Spider (78 x .4 = 31.2) goes to 31 and begins to close the web.

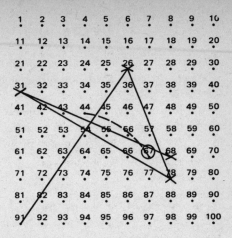

Caught in a pocket, fly (67 x .65 = 43.55) runs into the spider's line and must return to 67, losing his turn. Spider (31 x 2.2 = 68.2) extends his web to 68, creating a narrow wedge that limits the fly to just one move.

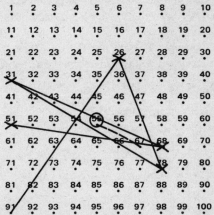

Fly's only move is to 55. Luckily that's where he lands (67 ÷ 1.22 = 54.918 032). His only chance to escape is if spider lands there too. But spider (68 x .75 = 51) moves to 51. He has captured the fly in only five moves.

The Big One

Involves: Two or more players, one calculator.

Object: To guess the number the "number giver" put into the calculator.

How to play: Somebody (the "number giver") secretly enters a three-digit number while the others have their eyes closed. The secret number is put in this way:

1. Key in the three digits
2. Press ÷ =

The other player, or players, are now allowed to see the display. All that shows is the big number 1. All the players (except the "number giver") take turns trying to guess the number that is in the calculator. Each enters a guess, then pushes the = key. Whoever guesses the number correctly will come up with a 1 on the display. If the person has not guessed the number, then the person's guess divided by the goal number will show on the display. This display is a clue the other players can use to tell how big the goal number is.

Caution: Do not push the Clear key at any time during this game—it will eliminate the secret number.

Sample Game

Wally, Carol, and Erin are playing. While Carol and Erin have their eyes closed, Wally secretly enters 374 ÷ =. The display shows 1.

Carol and Erin open their eyes, and take turns guessing the secret number.

	Keys In	Display Shows
Carol	700 =	1.871 657 7
Erin	200 =	0.534 759 3
Carol	400 =	1.069 518 7
Erin	380 =	1.016 042 7

(they know they're getting close now)

	Keys In	Display Shows
Carol	375 =	1.002 673 7
Erin	373 =	0.997 326 2

(just a bit too small)

	Keys In	Display Shows
Carol	374 =	1.

Carol is the winner. Since the display shows 1, then 374 must be the number Wally entered originally.

Variations

Easier: The "number giver" can use just a single-digit number like 8 for a little kid to guess. Playing with just two digits makes the game go faster, and is also easier.

Harder: Use a four-digit number to start off with. This is quite a challenge, and makes the players use the fourth and fifth decimal places in the answers they get as clues. And if you can guess a *five*-digit number in less than ten tries, you are an expert!

Crazy Nim

Involves: Two players and one calculator.

Object: To get to 27.

How to play: Players take turns adding a digit to the display until they get to 27. A turn consists of pressing a single digit key (not zero) and the + key. The first player to get to 27 wins.

The only catch is that a player may not push a key if that digit also appears on the display. For example, if the display shows 16, the player may not use either the 6 key or the 1 key.

As in regular NIM (see page 100), a player who goes over the goal number goes "bust" and loses.

Sample Game

The Nelsons can't make it for bridge, so Mom and Dad decide to play Crazy Nim. "Age before beauty," Dad quips and gets to go first.

	Keys	*Display Reads*
Dad	8 +	8
Mom	6 +	14

(Dad is cautious now, since the total after his turn will be within striking distance of 27.)

	Keys	*Display Reads*
Dad	3 +	17
Mom	8 +	25

(Dad wishes he could use the 2 to get to 27, but he can't since it's in the readout. There's nothing he can do now but make the only legal move open to him.)

	Keys	*Display Reads*
Dad	1 +	26
Mom	1 +	27

Mom wins, or rather, Dad loses. Next time Dad will make sure Mom can't get to that 25 number.

Variations

Easier: Play to 17 or to some other number smaller than 27.

Another interesting (and sometimes easier) variation is to allow players to go over the goal number. In that case, the player whose next turn it is must push – rather than + after he keys in his digit.

Harder: Play to a three-digit goal number, like 136, starting from 100.

Bullseye

Involves: Four to seven players, more or less, and one calculator.

Object: To hit the target number.

How to play: One player picks an easy-to-remember goal number, such as 1000 or 7777. Another player selects a number from 20 to 100 as a constant—that is, a number that's set to repeat the function assigned to it without having to be keyed each time. (Prime numbers like 37 or 53 make better constants in this case, because they are not easy to track and therefore more challenging than composite numbers.)

Here, the constant is keyed to multiply, thus: NUMBER x =. (This should fix the constant on most calculators. To check, key 10 x =, then 4 =. The calculator should read 40, or four times the constant number. If it doesn't, try varying the formula.)

Careful not to clear the calculator during the game, players take turns entering a guess and pushing the = key as they try to hit the bullseye. If the target number comes up with a decimal following it, the decimal is ignored. For example, if the target number is 7777, and a player hits 7777.83, that player is the winner.

Sample Game

Players agree on 5555 as the target number. Ray, who won the previous round, enters a constant of 97 x =. The display reads 9409.

Sequence	Input	Display Reads
Pam breaks the ice: 82.	82 =	7954
Carola says 75.	75 =	7275
Ray tries 67.	67 =	6499
Katherine: 59.	59 =	5723
Pam now tries 57.	57 =	5529
Carola, excited to be so close, calls for 57.3.	57.3 =	5558.1

(Now it's really close, and everyone is eager for one more chance. But it's Ray's turn.)

Ray goes for 57.28.   57.28 =   5556.16 (!)

Katherine is cautious. She doesn't want to underkey.

Her guess is 57.277.   57.277 =   5555.869

The decimal doesn't count, so Katherine is the winner. She takes the calculator and sets the constant for the next game.

Variations

Easier: Change the goal number to some easy-to-remember three-digit number like 500. The game is also easier to play with a two-digit constant like 25 or 60 than with a prime number like 17 or 31.

Harder: Set a five-digit goal number. Or use a three-digit constant, like 377. Or use both.

Mean Machine

Involves: Two or more players and a calculator for each.

Plus: Five pennies or similar markers for each player.

Object: To pick five numbers from the chart on the facing page which average the goal number.

How to play: Each player keys a number between 40 and 60 into his or her calculator. When everyone has a number on the calculator, one player adds them all up and divides by the number of players. The result is the goal number. If the average is 49.75, then 49 is the goal number.

Each player clears his or her calculator. On the first turn, each player picks a number from the chart, keys it into the calculator, and covers that number on the chart with a marker. On each of the next four turns, each player picks a number from the chart that is not covered, adds it to the display of his or her calculator, and then covers up the number picked.

When each player has had five turns, all of the players divide their totals by five. The player whose answer (the average of the five numbers) is closest to the goal number wins.

MEAN MACHINE NUMBER CHART

43	74	28	14
89	5	78	17
33	80	49	69
56	24	50	97
94	61	2	36
9	42	83	71

Reminder: Make sure each player covers the number he or she picked after each turn.

Sample Game

Nancy keys a number between 40 and 60 into her calculator, as does Sue. Their numbers are 44 and 59, which they add up to get 103. Dividing by 2, they get 51.5, which gives them a goal number of 51.

They both clear their calculators, and take turns picking numbers from the chart. After each turn, the number picked is covered with a penny.

Player	# Picked and Keyed		Totals	
Nancy	50		50	
Sue		56		56
Nancy	+ 43 =		93	
Sue		+ 17 =		73
Nancy	+ 49 =		142	
Sue		+ 89 =		162
Nancy	+ 42 =		184	
Sue		+ 5 =		167
Nancy	+ 61 =		244	
Sue		+ 83 =		260

Each player then divides the total on her calculator by 5. Nancy has 244 ÷ 5, for 48.8. Sue does 260 ÷ 5 =, giving her 52. Sue wins since she is closer to the 51 goal.

Variations

Easier: Each player picks only three numbers from the chart.

23

Harder: Players continue taking turns until every number on the chart is covered. Then each player divides by the number of turns he or she took. (This can be tricky if there are five or seven players, since not everyone will have the same number of turns.)

Calcu-break: Hinkey Pinkey

The answers to all the questions on this page are two rhyming words, like "mean bean" or "fat cat." If you can't guess the answer, work the formula on your calculator, then turn it upside down and read the answer. When you have the first word, *don't clear,* just continue with the number that is on your calculator.

What would you call fat fowl?

(1316 + 2222) x 10 _____ – 41 = _____

What's a pig puddle?

301 x 3 + 1 = _____ + 4 = _____

What's a large jam-session called?

51 x 18 = _____ + 1 = _____

If a bull met a cow, how would he greet her?

5.3 x 7.3 x .02 = _____ – .0004 = _____

What do you call the company owners' liabilities?

101 101 x 5 + 30 003 = _____ – 1 = _____

Instead of "God save the Queen!" what did supporters of Elizabeth I say?

(39 x 710 – 1) x 2 = _____ – 49 840 = _____

What's the surest way to catch a queen?

(808 x 8 – 37) x 5 = _____ ÷ 5 – 1089 = _____

Population

Involves: Two or more players, one calculator.

Object: To guess how big the population of a city, state, or country will be in ten years.

How to play: The players pick a city, say, and look up its population in a current world almanac (or other suitable reference). They then agree on a growth rate, or how fast they think the city is going to grow—2 percent or 5 percent or whatever. With the agreed-on estimate in mind, each player covertly writes down a guess as to how big the city will be in ten years.

The game proceeds as follows: The player keys in the growth rate constant (1.05 x =, for example, if the rate is estimated at 5 percent), then enters the current population of the city by the number of thousands; in other words, if the size of the city is 325 000, the appropriate entry would be 325. He now presses the = key ten times. The display in this case will show 529.390 71. Rounded off, the answer would be 529 (*thousand*), indicating how large the city will be in ten years.

The player whose guess comes closest to the projected answer is the winner and gets to select the city of Dnepropetrovsk for the next round.

Sample Game

Vera, having won the last game, picked a growth rate of 7% for Dayton, Ohio. Its size, as of the last census, was 262 332.

Here's how the guesswork went:

Wylie figured the city would grow by about 16 000 a year. For ten years that would be 160 000, so he wrote down 420 000 as his guess.

Vera thought Dayton would double in size in ten years, so she put down 520 001.

Ginnie guessed the growth would be about 100 000, so her total was 362 332.

Doug did some quick mental computations, then wrote down 605 312 as his estimate.

When all the guesses were on paper, Vera keyed 1.07 x = in the calculator. This put the growth rate in as a constant. She then put in the size of Dayton—262, signifying the number of thousands—and pushed = ten times. The display read 515.393 59, or 515 000 when rounded off to the nearest thousand.

Vera won again since her guess of 520 001 was closest to the result.

Variations

Simpler: Change the rate of growth to 10% or 20% to make the job of estimating the final size a bit easier.

Harder: Make the time period longer. It's easy to hit the = key 50 times instead of 10 times, but the game itself becomes considerably more complex.

Countdown

Involves: Two players, one calculator.

Object: To be the first player to get to zero.

How to play: One player keys in a two-digit number and covers the display so the other player doesn't know what the number is. The other player then keys in x, and a three-digit number, then pushes =. This provides the game's starting number.

Players take turns subtracting numbers from the display, but these numbers must derive from one of the digits already in the display. For example, if the display reads 205, the only numbers that may be subtracted are 222, 22, or 2 or 555, 55, or 5. It is illegal to subtract zero.

A player who subtracts and gets a negative number on the display loses.

The first player to get to zero wins.

Sample Game

Olin and Janet are watching TV, and during a commercial they pick up the calculator on the coffee table and play a quick game of Countdown.

Olin covers the display and keys in 55 while Janet looks the other way. Then while Olin turns his head, Janet keys in x 914 =. The result is 50 270, and Olin starts.

This game is adapted, with permission, from *Games With the Pocket Calculator,* by Sivasailam Thiagarajan and Harold D. Stolovitch, published by Dymax.

Olin	−22 222	=	28 048
Janet	−22 222	=	5826
Olin	−888	=	4938
Janet	−4444	=	494
Olin	−444	=	50

(Janet has only one legal move, and takes it.)

Janet	−5	=	45
Olin	−4	=	41
Janet	−4	=	37
Olin	−7	=	30
Janet	−3	=	27
Olin	−7	=	20
Janet	−2	=	18
Olin	−8	=	10
Janet	−1	=	9
Olin	−9	=	0

Olin wins. Janet, however, sees how she could have won when Olin gave her the calculator with 41 on it, and is ready to play another game during the next commercial break.

Variation

Simpler: Both players key in a two-digit number so the starting number will be smaller. Allow any player to use a "wild card," such as a 0 or a 5, as part of any number to be subtracted.

Tripoli

Involves: Two or more players and two calculators, one to keep the game going, the other for players to plot their moves.

Object: To get the display to show a triple, such as 444 or 777.

How to play: Play begins with the calculator clear. Players take turns adding or subtracting two-digit numbers. The numbers may not begin or end with zero.

Also: the two digits in the number may not be the same (numbers such as 33 or 88 are illegal); and the two digit keys may not be next to each other on the keyboard. If the first key in the number is 4, the next key can't be 1, 2, 8, or 7, since those keys border the 4 on the keyboard. (As you

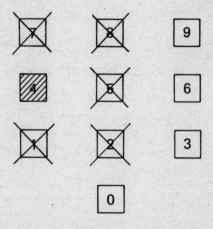

may have noticed, the digit 5 was omitted from the preceding group, and for good reason: it cannot be used in any circumstances because it is bordered by all the other legal keys.)

If a player makes the total on the keyboard go over 1000 or under zero, that player is out.

Sample Game

Denis starts out against Brian by keying 43.

Brian considers trying to get to 111, then realizes it won't work, since + 68 is the only number that can get him there, and the 8 corners the 6. So Brian keys + 82 =. The display reads 125.

Denis also considers 111, but there's no way. He would have to subtract 14, which is illegal because the digits 1 and 4 are keyboard neighbors. So he keys – 13 =, which puts the display at 112. (For the moment Denis is safe, because one digit is necessary to get to 111 and three digits to get to 222, and Brian must use a two-digit number.)

Brian decides to get away from 111, but he also wants to prevent Denis from coming back to it. So he keys in + 46 =. The display now reads 158.

Denis studies the keyboard. A – 47 would get him to 111, but that would be illegal because the 4 and the 7 are adjacent to each other. Then he sees something else, and his face lights up as he keys in + 64 =. The display shows 222, and it's Tripoli for Denis.

Brian's mistake was to use the + key. If he had done some checking, he might have realized that any two non-adjacent digits added to 112 would have allowed Denis to get to 222 legally. Brian's only option was to subtract.

Gotcha!

Involves: Two or more players, one calculator for each.
Plus: A deck of cards with all the face cards removed.
Object: To reach your goal number.

How to play: To determine his goal number, each player keys in a number of five or more digits with a decimal point after the second digit—such as 28.3947. This is followed by x and as many equal signs as it takes to overload the display. Thus, the result of "equaling out" 28.3947 would be 5.241 114 7. From this, the goal number would be determined simply by adding the first two-digit combination (52) and the last two-digit combination (47) for a total of 99. The player then writes his goal number on a slip of paper and conceals it from the others until the game is over.

The first player now clears his calculator and keys in 100, which serves as the general starting number. He draws a card from the top of the shuffled deck and places it, face up, beside the deck. The player may then either add, subtract, multiply, or divide by the face value of the card; or, if it suits his strategy, he may choose to pass. An ace may be counted as either 1 or 11. In the event a decimal crops up (as, say, when 100 is divided by 3), the decimal is simply dropped.

Players continue taking turns until the first player to reach his goal number calls out: "GOTCHA!"

Sample Game

Sherrie keys in 29.948 75 x = = etc., until the display overloads, showing 7.215 595 4. Her goal number is 72 + 54, or 126. Colin keys 61.376 x = = = =, getting 8.709 492 5. Since 87 and 25 are the first and last two-digit combinations, his goal is 87 + 25, or 112. Austin enters 81.3658 x and equals out to 35.662 311. His goal is 35 + 11, or 46.

All three jot down their goal numbers, which they conceal from the others. A shuffled deck of cards is on the table before them. They clear their calculators, then key in 100.

Sherrie begins and draws a 6. She places the card, face up, beside the deck, then adds 6 to her display, giving her 106 toward her goal of 126.

Colin goes next. He draws a 9, which brings his score to 109, three points shy of his goal.

Austin draws a 2, which, considering his low goal of 46, is a bit of luck. He keys in ÷ 2 and comes up with a 50, only 4 away from his goal.

An interesting outcome: For the next few turns both Colin and Austin continued to pass, neither of them drawing the one card they each needed to win (Colin a 3, Austin a 4). This gave Sherrie a chance to catch up, and now all she needed was a 9 to reach her goal. On her next turn she drew an ace. She could have passed, deciding to wait until she drew a 9. But she remembered that two 9's had already been discarded, thus reducing her chances. So Sherrie decided to add 1 to her display. This changed her magic number from 9 to 8, a card that no one had turned up yet.

Improving the odds paid off for Sherrie. Two turns later she drew an 8 and yelled "Gotcha!" to the surprise of her two opponents. Proving once again that it never hurts to give luck all the help it can get.

In the Chips

Involves: Two or more players, one calculator.

Plus: A pair of dice, a game board (see note), a marker for each player, 50 chips, and a bowl to hold the chips.

Object: To rake in the chips.

Note: Use the game board shown on the opposite page as a model for making a larger and more manageable copy. A quick and easy way is to copy it on one of those lined, yellow legal pads (8½" x 12½"), or on a lined sheet from a large notebook. With pencil and ruler, draw a heavy line on every other light line all the way down the page, and use the space at the top for additional lines as required. Vertical lines are drawn 1" apart. The dots appearing in certain boxes on the model indicate how many chips a player wins when he lands in any of those boxes.

How to play: Put all the chips in the bowl. (If poker chips aren't available, you can use pennies, buttons or paper clips.) Each player begins with his or her marker at 50. Roll the dice to determine who goes first, second, and so forth.

A turn consists of rolling the dice, then adding, subtracting, multiplying, or dividing the number you are on by the number on the dice. For example, if you are on 27 and roll a 4, you could do 27 + 4, 27 – 4, 27 x 4, or 27 ÷ 4. The resulting number tells you what box to go to. (If the result is a decimal, round it off to the nearest whole number.) In the example above, the player's best bet would be 27 ÷ 4, because he would land on 7, allowing him to take four chips from the bowl.

The game is over when all the chips have been taken.

	0	1	2	3	4	
5	6	7	8	9	10	11
12	13	14	15	16	17	18
19	20	21	22	23	24	25
26	27	28	29	30	31	32
33	34	35	36	37	38	39
40	41	42	43	44	45	46
47	48	49		50	51	52
53	54	55	56	57	58	59
60	61	62	63	64	65	66
67	68	69	70	71	72	73
74	75	76	77	78	79	80
81	82	83	84	85	86	87
88	89	90	91	92	93	94
	95	96	97	98	99	

Variations for In the Chips

(1) Each player starts with 30 chips, and anyone who lands in a payoff box receives the designated number of chips from each of the other players.

(2) Similar to variation (1), with the following provision: The player makes his move without the aid of the calculator and without saying how he made the move. The other players may use the calculator to monitor him. (Remember, he has four options open to him.) If he makes a mistake and goes to a wrong box, he must pay the other players three chips each.

Telling Times

Involves: Two or more players and one calculator.
Plus: Pencil and paper for scoring.
How to play: Each player writes down a two-digit number on a piece of paper so the other player(s) can't see it. When everyone has a number written down, all players turn their numbers over at the same time.

Within ten seconds each player has to write down an estimate of the product of the numbers. A player's score is the difference between his or her estimate and the answer when the numbers are multiplied together.

After ten turns, the player with the lowest total score wins.

Sample Game

Gene writes down the number 93, shielding it with her hand so Jason can't see it. Jason writes down 46 and turns it over. Then they show each other their papers.

Jason figures 90 x 50 is 4500, adds a bit and puts down 4508. Gene thinks 45 x 100, then subtracts seven 50's. This gives her 4500 − 350, or 4150, which she writes down barely in time.

Jason takes the calculator, and keys in 93 x 46 =. The answer is 4278. Since he's estimated 4508, he keys in 4508 − 4278 = and jots down a score of 230 for the round.

Gene calculates the difference between 4278 and her estimate, 4150, for a score of 128.

The person with the lowest total for ten turns wins.

Synergy

Involves: Four players in two teams of two each, one calculator.

Object: Each team tries to come closer to their goal number than the other team.

How to play: Each team writes down a number between 100 and 999 so the other team can't see it. They then fold the paper and give it to *one* member of the other team.

Only one member of each team looks at the goal number the other team has written down. After one person has looked at the goal number, members of the team take turns filling in the ovals with numbers. They can fill in the ovals in any order. After the ovals are all filled with numbers, the team members start filling the boxes with the function keys +, −, x, ÷, and =. When all the ovals and boxes are filled in, the team keys the number sentence they've created into the calculator. The team's score is the difference between the answer on the calculator and their goal number.

The team with the lowest score wins that round.

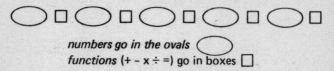

numbers go in the ovals ⬭
functions (+ − x ÷ =) go in boxes □

Sample Game

Bob and Eve are playing against Flo and Ben. Bob and Eve write down 657, fold the paper, and give it to Flo. Flo and Ben write down 329 and give it to Bob.

Flo and Ben go first. Taking turns, they write down numbers in the circles, as shown.

38

Then they take turns writing functions in the squares. Their final calculator sentence looks like this:

(37) [+] (58) [×] (19) [+] (346) [÷] (7) [=]

Bob and Eve then write numbers in the circles, like this:

(4) □ (115) □ (83) □ (16) □ (27) □

They take turns filling in the functions and get a final calculator sentence like this:

(4) [×] (115) [+] (83) [−] (16) [−] (27) [=]

When Flo and Ben do their calculator sentence on the calculator, they get 307.285 71. Since their goal number is 657, their score is 657 − 307.285 71, or 349.7142.

Bob and Eve key their sentence into the calculator, which shows the answer 500. Their goal number was 329, so their score is 171. Since Bob and Eve got the lower score, they win the round.

Minesweeper

Involves: Two players and a calculator. .

Object: For the captain to sweep all the mines off the sea in as few runs as possible.

How to play: One player places each of the 12 "mines" on a different number on "The Sea" (see facing page), spreading them out in such a way that the submarine must make extra runs to pick them up.

The sub captain then starts at zero and adds (or subtracts) a constant number that allows him to make measured stops during each run. Each time the captain pushes the = key, the display shows which number he is allowed to make a stop at. If there is a mine on that number, the captain picks it off the board.

At the end of a run the captain may, without penalty, go back along the same route by changing the *function sign* (+ or –) of his constant, in order to put himself in position for his next run, which begins when he changes his *number.*

The number of runs it takes the captain to pick up all the mines is his (or her) score. When all the mines are gone, the players swap roles. The captain who picks up all the mines in the least number of runs is the winner.

Note: It is illegal to use the number 1 as the constant for any run. Also, after a constant number has been used once, it may not be used again by the same captain during his turn.

If the calculator doesn't have a constant, just keep adding or subtracting the same number to the figure on the display.

"THE SEA"

0	1	2	3	4	5	6	7	8	9
10	11	12	13	14	15	16	17	18	19
20	21	22	23	24	25	26	27	28	29
30	31	32	33	34	35	36	37	38	39
40	41	42	43	44	45	46	47	48	49
50	51	52	53	54	55	56	57	58	59
60	61	62	63	64	65	66	67	68	69
70	71	72	73	74	75	76	77	78	79
80	81	82	83	84	85	86	87	88	89
90	91	92	93	94	95	96	97	98	99

THE MINES

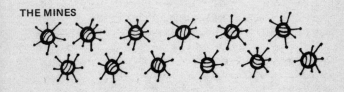

SUBMARINE

Sample Game

Mines have been laid by Susan at 11, 12, 17, 20, 24, 38, 43, 56, 68, 85, 93, and 97.

Starting at zero, Captain Augie makes his **first** run as follows:

+ 4 = = =	This takes him to 12; he picks up the mine.
= = =	He picks up the mines at 20 and 24.
= (eight times)	Now at 56, he gets that mine.
= = =	He scoops up the mine at 68.
= (seven times)	All the way to 96, where he stops to map out his strategy.

At the end of his first run, Augie has picked up five mines. He starts his **second** run by keying + 2 =. This moves him to 98 and places him in good strategic position for his **third** run:

– 5 =	He eliminates the mine at 93.
= (ten times)	He picks up the mine at 43.
=	Picks up another at 38.
= = = = = =	He's now at 8 and ready for his next sweep.

Keying the calculator to + 3, he sets out on his **fourth** run:

=	He wipes out the mine at 11.
= =	Gets the one at 17.
= (20 times)	Clear across the sea to 77.

He makes his **fifth** run:

+ 8 =	And gets the mine at 85.

Then launches his **sixth** run:

+ 12 =	To clear the last mine at 97.

(0)	1	2	3	(4)	5	6	7	(8)	9
10	⋈	(12)	13	14	15	(16)	17	18	19
(20)	21	22	23	(24)	25	26	27	(28)	29
30	31	(32)	33	34	35	(36)	37	38	39
(40)	41	42	43	(44)	45	46	47	(48)	49
50	51	(52)	53	54	55	(56)	57	58	59
(60)	61	62	63	(64)	65	66	67	(68)	69
70	71	(72)	73	74	75	(76)	77	78	79
(80)	81	82	83	(84)	85	86	87	(88)	89
90	91	(92)	93	94	95	(96)	97	98	99

This is what the ocean looks like at the end of Augie's first run. The X's are mines, the circles show where he stopped, and the circled X's indicate the mines he has picked up.

Augie has swept the ocean clear of mines in six runs. He now sets the mines up for Captain Susan to clear off.

A point of information: The captain of the sub can always get all of the mines off the board in 12 runs just by using a different number for each run. The challenge is to try to do better than 12 runs.

Variation

Harder version for hardier souls: Disallow the use of the numbers 1, 2, and 3 as constants. Also, score as an extra run any change in the function sign.

Fraction Fray

Involves: Two players and their calculators.

Plus: Six pennies or markers.

Object: To come closest in guessing the decimal equivalent of six fractions.

How to play: One player picks a fraction from the table (opposite), and each player secretly enters in his or her calculator the decimal he or she thinks is closest to that fraction.

After the players have keyed in their decimal estimates, they refer to the fraction and make the following entries: x denominator – numerator = ÷ denominator x =. (In case you've forgotten: in fractions the top number is the numerator and the bottom number is the denominator.)

The answer on the calculator is the person's score for that round. If the calculators have a memory, each player adds the result to the total score in memory. If score is being kept on paper, write the score for that turn under each player's name. Also, place a penny or a piece of cardboard over the fraction so it won't be picked again.

Players take turns picking fractions until six fractions have been used.

The player with the *lowest* score at the end of six turns wins.

1/5	5/8	1/3
3/8	1/6	4/6
9/10	5/9	8/9
1/10	3/4	3/5
4/5	4/9	7/10
2/9	3/10	7/8
1/4	5/6	1/2
2/3	7/9	2/5

Make sure you cover up each fraction with a
marker after it has been used

Recap: Pick a fraction, estimate its decimal equivalent,
and calculate your score according to the formula:

decimal estimate x denominator – numerator =
÷ denominator x =.

For example: If the fraction happens to be 9/12 and you
estimate its decimal equivalent to be .72, the formula would
be applied as follows: .72 x 12 – 9 = ÷ 12 x =. Your score
would then be .0009, indicating that your estimate was
slightly off. If you had correctly estimated .75, your score
would have been zero. And if you find yourself scoring too
many zeros with the fractions in the table above, a more
challenging assortment awaits you on page 47.

Sample Game

	Ellen's Score	Lana's Score

Ellen picks 1/6. Her decimal guess is .2, while Lana's estimate is .15.

		Ellen's Score	Lana's Score
Ellen keys	.2 x 6 – 1 = ÷ 6 = x =	.001 111 1	
Lana keys	.15 x 6 – 1 = ÷ 6 = x =		.000 277 7

Lana covers 1/6 with a penny, then picks 1/4. Ellen guesses .25; Lana .2.

Ellen keys	.25 x 4 – 1 = ÷ 4 = x =	0	
Lana keys	.2 x 4 – 1 = ÷ 4 = x =		.0025

After 1/4 is covered with a penny, Ellen picks 4/5. Ellen guesses 4/5 is .7. Lana figures 4/5 is .8.

Ellen keys	.7 x 5 – 4 = ÷ 5 = x =	.01	
Lana keys	.8 x 5 – 4 = ÷ 5 = x =		0

Lana covers up the 4/5 and picks 1/3. Ellen says .3; Lana guesses .33.

Ellen keys	.3 x 3 – 1 = ÷ 3 = x =	.001 111 1	
Lana keys	.33 x 3 – 1 = ÷ 3 = x =		.000 011 1

Ellen covers 1/3 and picks 7/10. Ellen thinks it's .7; Lana guesses .75.

Ellen keys	.7 x 10 – 7 = ÷ 10 = x =	0	
Lana keys	.75 x 10 – 7 = ÷ 10 = x =		.0025

Covering up 7/10, Lana picks 7/8. Ellen estimates .85; Lana thinks .6.

Ellen keys	.85 x 8 – 7 = ÷ 8 = x =	.000 625	
Lana keys	.6 x 8 – 7 = ÷ 8 = x =		.075 625
	Ellen's total score:	.012 847 2	
	Lana's total score:		.080 913 8

46

Since Ellen has the lower score, she is the winner. A .068 066 6 difference may not seem to be a very significant winning margin, but it counts a lot in a game like this.

Variation

Here's one for fraction-frayers who like to play rough:

FRACTION FRAY TABLE II

7/11	6/7	5/11
2/21	1/17	7/19
2/7	8/13	1/7
5/18	13/22	15/17
14/15	3/7	3/14
14/19	9/16	1/13
5/13	3/41	4/7

Reminder: After a fraction has been played, don't forget to cover it with a marker.

Trajectory

Involves: Two players, two calculators, and unclassified intelligence.

Object: To "blow up" your opponent's tank by estimating the trajectory of your shell so that it "hits" at the exact position of the enemy tank.

How to play: To understand how to play this game, it helps to visualize the arrangement:

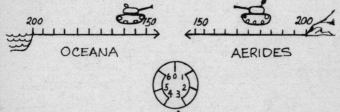

Represented above are the battlefields of two countries, Oceana and Aerides. A tank marker is positioned on each battlefield. In order for a player to "blow up" his opponent's tank, he must take into account the following:

1) The tank's field position.
2) Direction and speed of the wind.
3) Control numbers, which the player selects to determine his firing power.

At the beginning of the game each player places his tank anywhere along the battlefield of the country he is playing—Oceana or Aerides.

The next step is to determine wind speed and direction. Each side, in turn, rolls one of the dice. If both sides come up with the same number, the wind speed is zero, and the direction is toward Aerides. If they don't have the same number, then Aerides' throw determines wind *speed,* and his die is placed on the corresponding number of the wind speed indicator (shown on facing page).

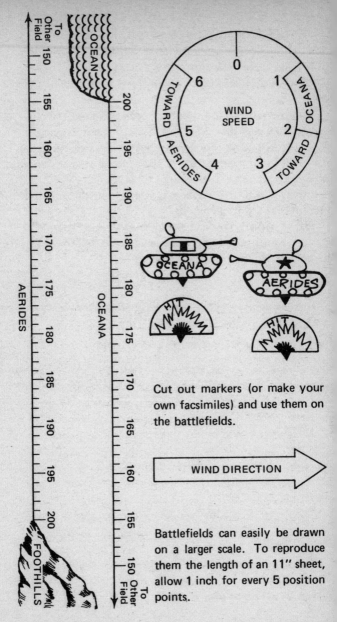

Cut out markers (or make your own facsimiles) and use them on the battlefields.

WIND DIRECTION

Battlefields can easily be drawn on a larger scale. To reproduce them the length of an 11" sheet, allow 1 inch for every 5 position points.

The number on Oceana's die determines the wind *direction.* If it is 4, 5, or 6, the direction is toward Aerides. If it is 1, 2, or 3, then the direction is toward Oceana. The dice are thrown to reestablish the wind speed and direction after every five turns.

Control numbers are selected. Each player picks a number, N (no higher than 20 in this case), and another number, K. (The N has a pronounced effect on the distance the shell will travel, whereas the K allows for greater precision when a player comes within range of his target.)

In any one turn, a player may change either N or K (but not both) to any other number.

Players take turns, and the one who rolled the higher number earlier goes first. If the wind is directed toward his battlefield, he fires his shell as follows:

$$N \times N + K - WIND - POSITION =$$

If the wind is directed toward the other battlefield: a + is substituted for the – before WIND, thus:

$$N \times N + K + WIND - POSITION =$$

During a turn, a player may, as a defensive tactic, decide to move his tank instead of shooting at his opponent's. In that event, the defending player rolls one die to determine how many notches forward or backward he may move.

After each player shoots (puts the formula through the calculator), he moves his "shell" to the spot that it hit, as indicated by the answer in the display. If the shell fails to hit the opposite battlefield, it is a wasted shot, and the other player takes his turn.

The first player to hit his opponent's tank wins.

Sample Game

Karen and David set up their tanks. Karen selects Oceana and puts her tank at 183. David, playing Aerides, places his tank at 157.

They each roll a die. Karen throws a 3 and David throws a 5. Since David is Aerides, he puts his die on the wind speed indicator, meaning that the wind is at 5 knots. Since Karen (Oceana) threw a 3, the wind is toward Oceana.

David goes first. He picks an N of 20 and a K of 1. The wind is away from him, so he keys

  20 x 20 + 1 + 5 − 157 = 249
  (his N) (his N) (his K) (wind)   (his position)

At 249 he is way off the board, and doesn't even bother to place his shell.

Karen goes next. She has picked an N of 15 and a K of 3. Since the wind is against her, she keys

  15 x 15 + 3 − 5 − 183 = 40
  (her N) (her N) (her K) (wind)   (her position)

Her shot is far too short.

David starts the second round. He changes his N to 18. Still using his original K of 1, David keys

  18 x 18 + 1 + 5 − 157 = 173
  (his N) (his N) (his K) (wind)   (his position)

David picks up his shell and puts it at 173—only 10 away from Karen's tank!

Karen decides she'd better move out of there. She throws a die and rolls a 5. She moves her tank 5 spaces back to 188. (She could have moved up, but that would have been even closer to David's shell.)

David changes his N to 19, again using a K of 1. He calculates:

$$19 \times 19 + 1 + 5 - 157 = 210$$

His shell is off the battlefield again!

Karen now takes a shot. She changes her N to 17. Her trajectory is:

$$17 \times 17 + 3 - 5 - 188 = 99$$

Still too short to hit the battlefield.

David changes his N back to 18. His shot is:

$$18 \times 18 + 1 + 5 - 157 = 173$$

Karen goes up to 19 for her N. Her shot comes to:

$$19 \times 19 + 3 - 5 - 188 = 171$$

She is getting close.

Now David changes his K instead of his N. He changes his K to 16, and fires:

$$18 \times 18 + 16 + 5 - 157 = 188$$

He moves his shell to 188, and blows Karen's tank off the battlefield on his fifth turn.

If the game had continued and the wind had changed, both players would have had to change their formulas—and perhaps their strategy as well.

Variations

Easier: Change the numbers on the battlefield so they are 15 to 20, instead of 150 to 200. Only let the tanks move to whole numbers.

Harder: Make up your own battlefield with higher numbers and more range. Let the wind speed change to the *sum* of the two dice thrown. Let a player move his tank *and* shoot every turn.

Over-the-Shoulder Bullseye

Involves: Two or more players and one calculator.

Object: To get to 555, either as a whole number or with decimal following. (The number 555.1294, for example, would be a winner.)

How to play: With the display of the calculator covered, each player secretly keys one (and only one) digit. With the display still covered, key in ÷ = = ÷ =. The display may now be uncovered. Since it reads 1, it doesn't provide any clues.

Players take turns keying in any number, then pushing the = key. The first player to get 555 (with or without a decimal) is the winner!

Caution: Do *not* push Clear key while game is in progress, or you will destroy the secret constant and never be able to get it back!

Sample Game

The calculator is cleared by Mike for the *only* time in the game. Then Mike covers the display with one hand and secretly keys in 2 with the other hand, so the rest of the players can't see him. Still covering the display, he lets Cammy key in her secret digit, which is 5. Now Pam covertly keys in 3, and Elmer follows with 8. With the display still covered (it now registers 2538), Mike keys ÷ = = ÷ =. The display is uncovered, showing 1, and giving no clue as to the secret constant.

The goal number is 555. Cammy starts.

Cammy	14	=	35 532.994
		(way too big!)	
Mike	.13	=	329.949 23
		(that's much better)	

Pam	.18	=	456.852 79
Elmer	.21	=	532.994 92
Cammy	.218	=	553.299 49

(fantastic guess!)

Mike	.2181	=	553.553 29
Pam	.219	=	555.837 56

Pam wins, since she got to 555 point something. She clears the calculator, covers the display, and puts in the first digit for the next game.

Skyhawk

Involves: Two pilots and their trusty calculators.

Plus: Pencil and paper.

Object: To shoot each other down.

How to play: In this game, each player is represented by a marker on the number chart. The markers can come from a Monopoly game or from a miniature chess set—anything that will stand up.

If the chart on the opposite page is too small for your markers, you can make a larger one simply by getting out a ruler, marking off 100 squares, and writing the numbers from 0 to 99 in them. (The chart can also be used for some of the other games.)

At the beginning of the game each pilot is allotted exactly 15 kilograms of "fuel." As fuel is used up, it should be crossed off or subtracted from the fuel supply list maintained by each.

Play starts with each player secretly keying a two-digit number into his calculator. To decide who goes first, players pick "odd" or "even," then show each other their starting numbers and put their markers on the board. If the total of their numbers is odd, the "odd" player goes first; likewise with even.

0	1	2	3	4	5	6	7	8	9
10	11	12	13	14	15	16	17	18	19
20	21	22	23	24	25	26	27	28	29
30	31	32	33	34	35	36	37	38	39
40	41	42	43	44	45	46	47	48	49
50	51	52	53	54	55	56	57	58	59
60	61	62	63	64	65	66	67	68	69
70	71	72	73	74	75	76	77	78	79
80	81	82	83	84	85	86	87	88	89
90	91	92	93	94	95	96	97	98	99

FUEL

15
14
13
12
11
10
9
8
7
6
5
4
———
3   (reserve tank)
2
1
0

FUEL

15
14
13
12
11
10
9
8
7
6
5
4
———
3   (reserve tank)
2
1
0

With each turn, a player gets a chance to shoot down his opponent. He makes a "shot" by multiplying or dividing by a number of his choosing. (It is illegal to multiply or divide by a number smaller than 1.) The whole number part of his "shot" is subtracted from the player's fuel. For example, if Jim is on 49 and takes a shot: $49 \div 5.39 = 9$ (which puts him on 9), then 5 is subtracted from his fuel.

If a player runs out of fuel, he becomes a "sitting duck" for the other player, who can shoot until he either hits the first player or runs out of fuel himself.

Sample Game

Peter secretly puts 47 on his calculator, while Rita enters 92 on hers. They both write down 15 to keep track of their fuel supply. Rita says, "Odd." They each show each other their numbers and place their markers on the board accordingly. Since $47 + 92 = 139$, and that's odd, Rita gets to start.

Rita keys $92 \div 1.04 =$, which puts her at 88 (she rounds off the answer 88.461 538 to the nearest whole number.) Rita subtracts 1 from her fuel supply.

Peter tries a shot, keying in $47 \times 1.75 =$, and subtracting one from his fuel supply. He's now at 82.

Rather than staying and fighting, Rita chooses to get away from 88. She keys $88 \div 5.92 =$, which gets her to 15. She's certainly a good distance from Peter, but it cost her 5 kg of fuel. She subtracts it, finding she only has 9 kg left.

Peter doesn't want to get within range, so he figures he'll jet down a bit from his 82. He keys: $82 \div 2.7 = 30$, and whoops! Without intending to, he has given Rita a great shot.

Rita, who was getting low on fuel, now has nothing to worry about. She gleefully keys in her position 15, then multiplies by 2 and pushes the = key. Peter groans. Thirty lights up on Rita's display—mission accomplished.

Moral: Calculate before you calculate.

Variations

Easier: Allow each pilot more fuel at the beginning of the game, so he'll have more time to pursue his opponent.

Harder: If one player is winning consistently, there are ways to make the game harder for him, easier for the other person. One way is to give him less fuel at the beginning and to let the other player have more fuel. Another handicap is to restrict the better player to a starting number below 20. This means that he will have to use up a good bit of fuel to get the other person, especially if the other person ends up at a large number like 97 or so.

More players: It is easy to play with more than two players. This can be done by setting up two or three teams of two players each. Or the game can be a free-for-all, with each player trying to shoot down any of the others.

Calcu-break: unQuotable Quotes

The answers to all of these questions are familiar pairs of words. If you can't think of the answers, simply work out the formula after each question on your calculator and write the words in the appropriate blanks. Do not clear your calculator after you've done the first word—continue with your answer to get the second word.

What would you call a couple of pot-smoking guys who had just stood up their dates:

117 x 42 =_____ x 11 + 3280 =_____

What does Caspar the ghost say when he answers the phone?

.2 x .2 x .2 =_____ ÷ 2 =_____

What would tell the world the Devil got married?

45654 + 12120 − 40 =_____ + 4 =_____

What did Br'er Fox do to catch Br'er Rabbit?

6 x 53 − 1 =_____ − 316.3 =_____

GAMES FOR ONE PERSON

Some of the Games of Chance can be played by your-self—Doubles and Craps and the Poker games can all be played alone. But there are other games which are just challenges for a person that are pretty much irrelevant to any other people who might be around. These are presented here as games for one person.

The games have the same appeal as Solitaire. The challenge of playing them, of solving the problem, of trying for a better solution is just as satisfying in its own dimensions as climbing a mountain or inventing a new automobile engine. There is the same sense of quest, of achievement, of reaffirmation of a person's powers of wit and determination.

If you find any particularly ingenious solutions, or have some one-person games that you enjoy doodling with, please send them to Wallace Judd, care of Warner Books, 75 Rockefeller Plaza, New York, New York, 10019.

Maze

Involves: One or more players and a calculator.

Object: To get through the maze with the most points on your calculator.

How to play: Start at the top of the maze (at right), choose your path, and work your way down, section by section, tracing a continuous path to the bottom. Every move must be either across or down. No upward moves are allowed, and you can't retrace a line.

Every time you go along a line, follow the instruction indicated for that line. Try to choose the path that enables you to score the *most* points on your calculator.

Calculator note: If your calculator has algebraic power logic, as with the Texas Instruments SR 30, then you will need to push the = key after each operation.

THE MAZE

Start here

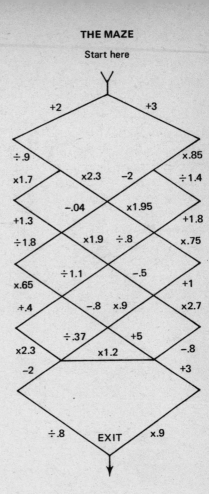

Total = _____

Variation

After going for high score, try this variation for size: See if you can go through the maze with a score as *low* as possible. This time it is permissible to go up as well as down, but you can't go along the same line twice.

Sample Game

Here is how one player came through with a score of 14.609 699. You should be able to double that. And if you're a maze whiz you should be able to do even better. (To find out, compare your score with that on page 124.)

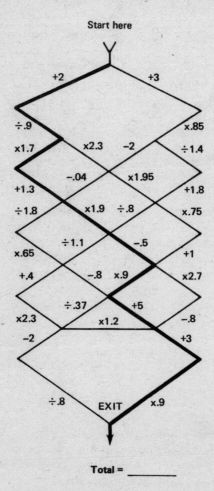

Start here

+2   +3

÷.9   x.85

x1.7   x2.3   −2   ÷1.4

−.04   x1.95

+1.3   +1.8

÷1.8   x1.9   ÷.8   x.75

÷1.1   −.5

x.65   +1

+.4   −.8   x.9   x2.7

÷.37   +5

x2.3   x1.2   −.8

−2   +3

÷.8   EXIT   x.9

Total = _____

Solitaire

Involves: A player and a calculator.

Object: To go from a given number to the goal number in the fewest strokes using certain keys only.

How to play: Each game has a goal number and a limited set of keys that are permitted to be used. A typical set of specified keys would be + − x ÷ = and 4. The goal number might be 27. The player could then do anything with the legal keys to get to the goal number. In this case, one might do 44 ÷ 4 + 4 + 4 + 4 + 4 =, which comes to 27. For some calculators, there are even shorter solutions. The answers at the back of the book will work for most calculators. The important thing is to find the shortest solution on *your* calculator, and not worry about the shortest way on somebody else's.

The example above takes 13 keystrokes. There is an even shorter solution taking only 10 strokes. Can you figure it out? To check your answer, see page 124.

Following are four sets of Solitaire puzzles. Groups I, II, and III are arranged in order of increasing difficulty. Group IV varies slightly in that there are no starting numbers.

Group I: Problems to start with

Start At	Use Any of These	To Get To	In ( ) Strokes
91	7, 4, +, −, x, ÷ and =	21	6
3	5, 9, +, −, x, ÷ and =	32	5
4	6, 3, +, −, x, ÷ and =	19	5
13	5, 7, +, −, x, ÷ and =	58	6
72	2, 8, +, −, x, ÷ and =	20	7
64	1, 6, −, x ÷ and = (*without* the + key)	48	7

65

Group II: Moderately difficult

Start At	Use Any of These	To Get To	In ( ) Strokes
9	8, 7, +, −, x, ÷ and =	14	4
12	4, 5, x, ÷, = and .	50	5
10	7, 9, +, x, ÷, = and .	73	9
31	7, 8, +, x, = and .	56	7
5	6, 7, +, −, x, ÷ and =	69	6

Group III: Toughies

These puzzles should really stretch your imagination. None of them involve a constant for addition or subtraction. (If you use a Casio calculator, the double keystrokes x x or ÷ ÷ needed to fix the constant for multiplication or division may be counted as a single keystroke.)

Start At	Use Any of These	To Get To	In ( ) Strokes
2	5, 4, −, x, ÷ and =	77	10
4	9, 7, +, −, x, ÷, = and .	62	7
1	3, 9, −, ÷ and =	256	10
2	5, +, x, ÷ and =	27	7
8	3, 7, +, −, x and =	199	10
4	1, 6, +, x, ÷ and =	100	9

Group IV: Starting from nowhere

Using only the keys 3, +, -, x, ÷, = and ., get to 110 in six moves. Notice that you are allowed to use the decimal point key.

This solitaire puzzle is very negative. Using only the keys 8, -, ÷ and =, get to 424 in thirteen keystrokes.

Using only 8, +, -, x, ÷ and =, get to 49 in seven keystrokes.

If you can do this one in nine moves, you're pretty good at solitaire. If you can do it in eight moves, you're an expert! Using only 7, +, -, x, ÷, = and ., go to 100. Again, notice that you are allowed to use the decimal point.

This problem requires an addition constant—allow for extra keystrokes if you don't have one on your calculator. Using only 6, 8, +, -, x, ÷ and =, get to 936 in ten moves.

The Labyrinth

Involves: One or more players and a calculator.

Object: To go through the labyrinth with the *lowest* score.

How to play: Trace a continuous path through the labyrinth, as in the MAZE. There are a few differences in the rules, however:

In the LABYRINTH you *are* allowed to move upward as well as downward. You may also go along a line you've been on before—but only after you have gone to another segment. In the illustration below, the player has just covered the segment marked -.9. But he can't go back up -.9 right away. He has to take a detour. If he went up x1.4, back across +1.9, and down ÷1.8, he could then go down -.9 again.

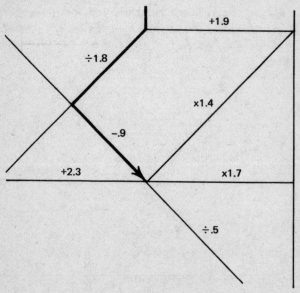

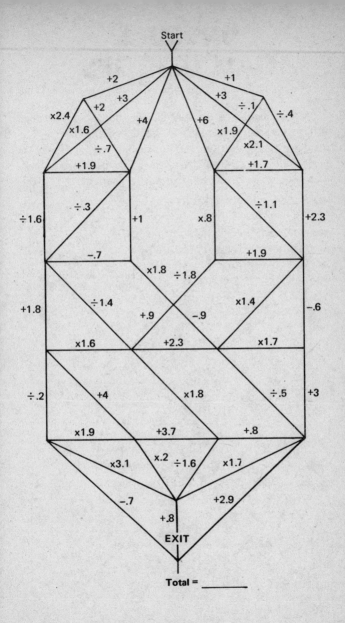

Start

Total = _____

UNUSUAL CALCULATORS

All the calculators on the following pages are from the author's personal collection (except the SPEECH PLUS™ calculator). The information included was gathered in spring, 1977, and availability of any of the calculators from the sources mentioned can in no way be guaranteed.

The Talking Calculator: Speech Plus^{TM}

It talks! It's hard to believe your ears the first time you hear the SPEECH+ calculator telling you out loud the names of the keys you just pushed. In addition to the numbers, the calculator tells you what function (+, -, x, or ÷) you keyed, as well as "percent," "root," "clear," and "point," "store," and "on" (memory).

The key under the = key is supposed to show a speaker, and when you push it, the calculator repeats aloud whatever is on the display. The dark key under the repeat key is the silent key, which allows you to use the calculator silently, if necessary. The full address of Telesensory Systems is 1889 Page Mill Road, Palo Alto, California 94304.

CheckMaster™: The Checkbook Calculator

The CheckMaster™ is not a hand calculator that is slim enough to fold into your checkbook. It is a unique, self-contained plastic checkbook with a built-in calculator that always remembers your balance! That's right. You deduct your check, turn it off, and the next time you're at the bank, simply turn it on and there's your correct balance. The keys are not marked +, -, or x; instead, the keys read CHECK, DEPOSIT, BALANCE, and CLEAR. When you have made out a check, you simply enter the amount of the check into the display and push CHECK. The amount is subtracted from your balance, and your balance is displayed. For a deposit, enter the amount and push DEPOSIT. The most convenient feature of the calculator is that you don't have to key in your balance each time you want to deduct a check or enter a deposit. The calculator remembers it.

Unfortunately, this calculator is not being produced any longer.

The Overhead Demonstration Calculator

   This unusual calculator was designed by the author to allow him to make demonstrations to classes and large audiences. By moving the projector away from the screen, digits over 50 cm tall (about a foot and a half) can be shown! This four-function, memory calculator is indispensible for demonstrating calculator games, tricks, or functions to groups larger than four or five. It is available from Stokes Publishing, Box 415, Palo Alto, California, 94302.

The CASIO micro-mini is a miniature calculator with a full-sized range of functions. It has eight-digit readout, constants for multiplication and division, and an easy-to-read liquid crystal readout. A little thicker than a box of wooden matches, the micro-mini is powered by a battery about the size of an aspirin—the same sort of battery that powers electric watches. Despite the miniature size, the keys are separated well enough to allow the user to push them adequately.

The CalcuPen™ Calculator

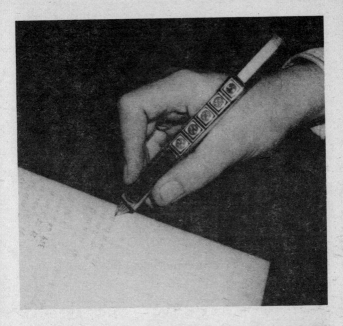

It's a real gimmick—an eight-digit calculator in the case of a ballpoint pen that actually writes. A rather expensive (around $85) toy for the affluent executive or calculating used-car salesman, the CalcuPen has keys that are unique. Each key has four functions. If you roll your finger off the key in the proper direction, the function on that part of the key is executed. It takes a little getting used to and is never quite as fast as a standard keyboard, but it can be quite accurate—surprisingly. The digits in the readout are about the size of those in a standard TI-1200 or HP-25; they're small but legible. The pen cartridge is only as long as a match—evidently designed to accommodate the check-writer more than the novelist. The CalcuPen is available from Chafitz, Box 2188, Dept. 592, Rockville, Md. 20852.

The Fraction Calculator: Casio AL-8

You want a calculator that will tell you the answer to 3/9 + 2/8 + 1/3, as a fraction and in lowest terms? Then consider the CASIO AL-8. It not only will do the problem—it will reduce each fraction to lowest terms as it is entered. The answer will be shown as 11/12. At the push of a key, the answer will be converted into a decimal, so if you want that decimal equivalent, you don't have to key the fraction in again. The AL-8 also will work with improper fractions, so you can do 3 1/7 - 2 3/4, again with the answer in lowest terms. Or it can mix improper and proper fractions in the same problem. It also gives the answer to division problems in terms of a whole number quotient and an integer remainder. So if you want 23 ⟌ 347 , the answer shown on the calculator is 15. Push the special key for remainders, and the remainder 2 is displayed.

And as a grand finale, this versatile calculator allows you to compute in hours, minutes, and seconds in that form, without having to convert to decimal equivalents.

The MICKEY MATH Calculator

This calculator, with its carrying handle, six-digit display, and offset key labels, was designed especially for young children. The philosophy behind the offset key labels appears to have been that if the digits are printed directly on the keys themselves, as on most calculators, a child must cover up the number in order to press the key. Hence, a child could be uncertain about the key he or she pressed, since it is covered up while being pressed. In actual fact, this has not been a problem with children I've worked with, at least by the ages of five or six.

The calculator producers were not content with a MICKEY MATH calculator, (which appears to have been originally produced by Omron with a shorter display than their 86) and so produced a MICKEY MATH adaptor, as well as curiously wrapped MICKEY MATH batteries.

The Accurate Calculator: Sheen

The most unusual feature of this Malaysian-assembled calculator (aside from its instantly-recognizable, large keys) is its incredible accuracy. With only an eight-digit display, it's a sleeper. Suppose you try the problem .000 003 ÷ 800 000 = on a normal calculator. The answer is zero— or at least it appears to be—because it is too small for the calculator to show you. On the Sheen calculator, the answer also appears to be zero. But if you multiply the answer (which shows zero on the display) by 10, then by 10 again, and so on, eventually a .3 peeks out, followed by a .37 and finally a .375—the basic answer. If you keep track of the number of times you multiplied by 10, you know the place value of the answer, too.

Another quirk of the calculator that brings you up short a bit the first time you notice it is the way it enters an integer. If you want to enter 496, you clear the calculator and get a right-justified 0. So far so good. Then you key in the 4, and the display shows 00000004! Key in the 9, and it now shows 00000049. After keying in 6, it gives 00000496. Push the + key, and all the zeros disappear, leaving you with just 496 showing on the display!

GAMES OF CHANCE

The games in the following section do not depend on skill at all—it's luck that makes them fun. The smallest child and the most profound mathematician meet on common ground here, as long as the child is able to count pairs, match digits, and tally his score.

These games are similar to most card or table games in that they serve simply to bring people together to interact for fun.

None of the games take any calculator more complicated than a simple, four-function-plus-constant that is for sale everywhere for less than $15, with adapter. Like most card games, these games require that you have a score pad and pencil. All of them require one calculator for each player. And although you could play passing a calculator from one player to the next, the games would be less interesting that way. It would be like dealing to one player at a time in cards, and having each individual play his hand without seeing what the others are doing.

Doubles

Involves: Two or more players, one calculator for each.

Object: To get "doubles" (two of the same digit in a row), "triples" (three in a row), or "quads" (four in a row).

How to play: Each player makes up a number, such as 2.735 486 1, then pushes x. Players then take turns pushing = five times and checking each new number in the display for points. Points are scored as follows: 1 point for each double, 2 points for each triple, and 4 points for each quad. The player with the highest score after five turns is the winner.

Note: The number a player makes up at the beginning may not start with zero. Nor may it contain any doubles or triples. For instance, 3.477 281 is not permitted, because of the double 7.

What are the chances of getting a triple as compared to getting a double? Or the odds against coming up with a quad? See page 126 for some eye-opening probabilities.

Sample Game

Suzie thought she was luckier than Jan. So they played a game of doubles to see who was luckier.

Suzie keyed in 8.397 841 2. She then pressed x and pushed = five times. These were her results:

8.397 841 2 x = 70.523 736   (no doubles)
                    = 592.247 13   (double 2's — 1 point)
                    = 4 973.597 3   (no doubles)
                    = 41 767.48   (no doubles)
                    = 350 756.66   (triple 6's — 2 points)

Suzie's score was just three points.

Jan keyed in 3.971 371 5. Here were her results:

$$3.971\ 371\ 5 \times = 15.771\ 791 \quad \text{(a double } 7-1 \text{ point)}$$
$$= 62.635\ 641 \quad \text{(no doubles)}$$
$$= 248.749\ 39 \quad \text{(no doubles)}$$
$$= 987.976\ 23 \quad \text{(no doubles)}$$
$$= 3\ 923.223\ 5 \quad \text{(double 2's} - 1 \text{ point)}$$

Jan scored a mere two points.

Suzie beat Jan by a point, so her luck was a shade better.

Optional rule: Not to suggest that anyone would even think of "loading the dice" in this game—there's always the possibility of an experienced player subconsciously remembering a few high-scoring numbers from previous games and having an advantage over less experienced players. To offset such a possibility, an alternate method for assigning numbers may be requested by any player. One way would be for players to swap calculators and put in the last four or five numbers.

Mean Bean

Involves: Three or more players, one calculator.

Plus: Pencil and paper for each player.

Object: To guess what the mean of all the numbers will be.

How to play: Each player secretly writes down two numbers smaller than 100, and bigger than 1. One number is a whole number, like 55 or 37. This number will be added to the numbers of the other players, then divided by as many players as there are to get the mean.

The second number a player writes may have a decimal part, such as 55.12 or 64.333. This number is circled. It is the player's "bean," his guess as to what the mean will be when all the players' numbers are averaged.

After everyone has made his or her selections, all the numbers are revealed. Those that are not circled are added on the calculator, and divided by the number of players. The person whose "bean" is the closest to the mean (another term for the average) is the winner.

Make sure that players cross out the old numbers before the next round begins.

Sample Game

Here's how Able, Baker, Charlie and Dan got their means and "beans" together:

	Able	Baker	Charlie	Dan
Number	38	92	44	76
Guess	(48.2)	(50)	(58.3)	(65)

They added up their numbers, 38 + 92 + 44 + 76 = and divided by 4. The answer was 62.5. Dan's guess of 65 was the closest to 62.5, so he won.

The next round, Able did some thinking. He had a hunch that Baker and Dan were likely to guess low and give low numbers next time—and that he might be able to make the average really low. So he wrote down a very low "bean" and number.

Baker also figured the others might average lower than the 62.5 of the preceding game, so he kept his guess in the 50's.

Charlie didn't seem to do any thinking at all.

And Dan decided to go low and guess high. Here are each player's numbers and their circled guesses:

	Able	Baker	Charlie	Dan
Number	3	32	57	27
Guess	(33)	(54)	(48)	(63)

The average was 3 + 32 + 57 + 27 ÷ 4 = 29.75. Able's thinking paid off, and he was the winner with the lowest (and closest) guess.

Calculator Poker

Involves: Three or more players, one calculator for each.
Object: To get the best poker hand.

How to play: Each player keys a number on his calculator that must be larger than 6.4 and smaller than 10. Only one decimal place of the number is keyed in by the player, who then covers the display and lets two other players each key in two digits. The player then pushes x = = = =. Each push of the = key is another "card," and can be bet on. The final "hand" consists of the five digits to the left of the decimal point on the calculator display.

The winning hand can be determined by referring to the chart shown below. If two players have hands with the same precedence, then the player with the highest cards wins. For example, if two players each have a pair, the highest pair wins. If two players each have a straight, the straight with the highest card in it wins.

Players' options: The digit 1 may also be played as an ace, the highest card; and the digit 0 may also be played as a ten.

Precedence of Hands: Calculator Poker

Hand	*Example*	
Five of a kind	11111	
Odd "flush"	51937	(contains 13579 in any order)
Even "flush"	80624	(contains 02468 in any order)
Four of a kind	88838	
Straight	95786	(contains 98765 or any se-
Full house	47744	quence in any order)
Three of a kind	20622	
Two pair	59795	
One pair	38568	

(See Solutions, page 127, for an explanation of the probabilities underlying this chart.)

Sample Game

Zoe and Donna and Odie got together for poker one night. When they found the deck had only 51 cards, they played with calculators instead.

Each covered up the display of her calculator, and entered a number from 6.5 to 9.9. Here's what they entered:

Zoe	Donna	Odie
8.3	6.9	9.2

Then they passed their calculators (with the display covered) to their left, and when they got them back, this is what they read:

Zoe	Donna	Odie
8.349	6.992	9.204

Passing their calculators (covered) to their right, they got them back like this:

Zoe	Donna	Odie
8.34985	6.99294	9.20473

Making sure the others didn't see the results, each of the women keyed $x = = = =$. Now their hands looked like this:

Zoe	Donna	Odie
40587.599	16722.414	66077.752

Zoe had 40587, which is nothing. Donna had 16722 for a pair of 2's. And Odie had 66077, good for two pair. Odie won hands down.

Craps

Involves: Two or more players, one calculator.

Object: Same goal as in regular craps. Try to "get" a seven or eleven on the first "roll." If you don't do that, then try to roll your point before a seven or eleven comes up.

How to play: One player handles the calculator. He is the "roller." The others then simply bet on his or her play.

The "roller" starts by picking a random number from zero to nine, one like 6.339 478. He then keys x =. The number farthest to the right in the display is his "point," unless he rolls a 7 or an 11, in which case he wins. If the last two digits are 12, this counts as a 12 and not as a 2.

The "roller" continues playing by pushing the = key and checking the last two digits on the right. If a 7 or an 11 comes up, the roller loses or "craps out." If it's the same number as his point, the roller wins.

Note: A final digit of zero, with a 1 in front of it, counts as a 10. If the final digit is zero and does not have a 1 just before it, it counts as a zero, and the person's point is a zero.

Sample Game

Jerry Lee was hot — he didn't care whether he played on the calculator or with the bones. The people gathered round to see how he'd do and to bet on his roll.

Jerry started by keying in 3.489 216 7 x =. This gave him 12.174 633, so his point was 3, the last digit in the display. (If he'd had 7 as the last digit, or 11 as the last two digits, he would have won on the first roll.) As he pushed = to try to get his point (3), these were his results:

$$= \qquad 42.479\ 932$$
$$= \qquad 148.221\ 68$$
$$= \qquad 517.177\ 56$$
$$= \qquad 1804.544\ 5$$
$$= \qquad 6296.446\ 8$$
$$= \quad 21\ 969.667$$

Since the last digit of the display was a 7, Jerry lost.

Calculator Bingo

651	1029	1599	1711	2501
2891	1989	1131	779	589
551	1209	3009	1911	969
2989	1071	1891	2419	1769
609	931	3111	1829	861

1989	609	1209	2501	931
1829	3009	2989	1029	1891
861	651	1071	1711	3111
1769	969	1911	589	2891
2419	551	779	1599	1131

Calculator Bingo

Involves: Two or more players and one calculator.

Plus: 75 markers to cover numbers on the board. They can be lima beans or small chips or pennies — anything small that won't slide.

Object: To get five markers in a row on your board. The row can be across, down, or diagonal.

How to play: Each player picks a game board (from opposite or following page), and takes a handful of markers.

Players then decide the order in which they will take turns.

Numbers called are determined by the factor list below.

The first player picks two numbers from the factor list — one from the left side and one from the right side. The player multiplies these two numbers on the calculator and reads out the answer. All players then find the answer on their board and cover it with a marker.

Players keep taking turns picking factors and multiplying them and reading out the answer until somebody has five markers in a row.

Factor List	
31	21
29	39
49	19
51	59
41	61

Multiply any factor on the left
by any factor on the right

2891	589	2501	1131	1071
2419	3111	609	861	1209
1829	1911	969	931	1769
1599	779	651	551	3009
1711	1989	1029	1891	2989

969	551	1711	2501	1891
1029	2891	1599	651	2419
3111	1829	931	1989	609
2989	861	1209	1769	1911
589	3009	1131	1071	779

Variation

If you are playing with a large group, you can have each player make up his or her own board. Hand out copies of the blank board below, and ask each player to write a number in any blank cell on his or her board. The distribution of numbers should be more or less random. These are the numbers to use:

2501	609	1829	931	1989
1769	861	3009	1209	2891
1891	779	1029	551	1071
1711	651	589	1131	969
2419	2989	3111	1599	1911

Error Declarer

Involves: Two or more players, one calculator.

Object: For the others to figure out the mistakes the "error declarer" is making.

How to play: For the first round, one person is chosen to be the "error declarer." He decides on a mistake that he will consistently make, such as pushing the 2 key every time the digit 8 occurs in a problem, or pushing the ÷ key every time the + key is intended. Of course, the "error declarer" doesn't tell anyone what mistake he's going to make, and makes sure that nobody can see him keying in the problems.

The other players take turns giving problems to the "error declarer." He works them out, making sure that nobody sees the keys he pushes. Then he shows the answer to all the other players.

The other players try to figure out what mistake the "error declarer" is making. The first one to tell what the error is wins the round, and gets to be the "error declarer" in the next round.

Sample Game

Bob, Shelley, Larry and Sue were tired of bridge, so they stopped for a while, and Bob began toying with the calculator they had been using. That's when he decided to have a little fun and rope the others into another game—without letting them know it was a game. "That's funny," he said, "there seems to be something wrong with this thing. Looks like one of the keys has gone haywire."

Sue looked up in surprise. "Really?"

"Give me some problems, and I'll show you what I mean," Bob said.

(Bob decided that whenever the number 6 was given, he'd put in 66.)

Sue said, "348 x 256."

Bob keyed in 348 x 2566, and answered, "892968."

Larry said, "107 + 99."

Bob keyed in 107 + 99 =, and said, "206."

(Now Larry, Sue, and Shelley knew that the "haywire" key wasn't 1, 0, 7, 9, or +.)

Shelley tried, "84 – 62."

Bob keyed in 84 – 662 =, giving "negative 578."

Sue guessed something was fishy with the 62, since the answer was such a big negative number. So she said, "Try 6 + 2." Bob keyed in 66 + 2, and that was when Sue caught him in the act and realized what was really fishy. "I think somebody's trying to double-six us," she announced.

Bob grinned and hander her the calculator. "Your turn," he said.

Variations

Easier: Change a digit key to another digit key. For example: 7 becomes 9. Thus, 3977 + 9172 becomes 3999 + 9192.

Eliminate a digit altogether: remove any 5's. Then 3850 x 215 becomes 380 x 21.

Change one function to another function: E.g., + becomes x, and 47 + 32 becomes 47 x 32.

Change one digit in the readout to another digit: E.g., 1 in the readout becomes 7, so 9185 would become 9785 — in the readout.

Harder: Change the sign of the first number: E.g., 47 + 39 becomes −47 + 39 =.

Change any digits after the first two to 8's: E.g., 3947 ÷ 2904 becomes 3988 ÷ 2988 =.

Change a digit to a decimal point. E.g., 4 becomes decimal point. 3492 − 408 becomes 3.92 − .08.

Reversie

Involves: Two players and one calculator.

Object: To reverse the digits on the calculator by adding or subtracting just one number.

How to play: One player puts a repeater on the calculator—a number like 12121212 or 737373. He then hands the calculator to the other player, who has one minute to figure out a number to add to (or subtract from) the display in order to reverse the digits. If the digits are 737373, the addition (or subtraction) has to change them to 373737.

Sample Game

David put in the number 17171717, then gave the calculator to his wife, Karen, saying, "Honey, the way you get things backwards, this should be easy for you."

Without gracing his comment with a reply, she pushed the + key, thought for a while, then keyed in 54545454 =. When the calculator display showed 71717171, she handed him the results and cooed, "Living with your attitudes has made a lot of things backwards."

Variations

Simpler: Put in smaller numbers to reverse—such as 8181 or 2929. Or give the person who's trying to reverse the digits two tries. Change the time limit to two minutes.

Harder: Limit the reversal process to one function — either addition or subtraction. Shorten the time limit to 30 seconds — or to 10 seconds for experts!

Crypto

Involves: Two or more players, one calculator each.

Object: To get closest to the two-digit goal number by using four random digits and any functions on the calculator.

How to play: One player keys in a number from 33 to 99 without showing it to the others. With the display covered, a second player keys x, inputs another number from 33 to 99, then keys =. The number in the display is noted on a sheet of paper.

Now push ÷ = =. Add the number you had in your display earlier. The first four digits of the display are the digits you use to try to get to the goal. The last two digits in the display are your goal number.

Every player tries to figure out on his or her own calculator how to combine the four digits to get to the goal. Any of the functions can be used, and players can combine digits into larger numbers. If the numbers were 3927 and the goal was 25, then 29 – 7 + 3 = would be a winning move.

Note: Rounding off is allowed. If the given digits are 3497 and the goal is 19, it would be legal to give 4 ÷ 3 x 9 + 7 = as the answer, even though the answer on the calculator is 18.999 999.

Also, every digit must be used once, and only once, in the solution.

Sample Game

Dale keys in his number (from 33 to 99) without showing the others. He keys in 48. With the display covered, Brad secretly keys in x 91 = (his number from 33 to 99). They look at the answer, 4368, and Margot, who is also playing, writes it down. They push ÷ = =, and add 4368, which gives them 4368.0002. The four digits they are to use are 4, 3, 6, and 8, and their goal number is 2.

96

Brad tries 6 x 4 ÷ 8 - 3 = and gets 0.

Margot tries 8 x 4 ÷ 6 - 3 = and gets 2.333 333 3 — very close!

Dale tries 8 x 4 ÷ 6 ÷ 3 = and gets 1.777 777 7 — the same distance away as Margot!

Brad, trying something a bit unorthodox, tries 63 ÷ 8 ÷ 4 =, which gives 1.968 75. Since neither Dale or Margot can come closer to 2, Brad is the winner.

Variations

Easier: Allow parentheses to be used, and work out partial solutions. If you had 1673 and a goal of 27, the solution (7 x 3) + (1 x 6) would be legal.

Another way to make the game easier is to set a time limit. For instance: the one closest to the goal number in five minutes wins.

Harder: Don't allow combinations of digits. For example, 39 - 27 would be an illegal solution if each digit has to be used separately.

Amazing Maze

A section of the silicon-chip brain of a typical calculator magnified several hundred times, shows the complex arrangement of the transistor network. A single chip may contain up to 10,000 transistors. To make a circuit this tiny, a large blueprint is first drawn up to exacting standards. The drawing is then reduced photographically and finally "etched" into the crystalized, polished silicon chip.

KIDDIE CORNER

The games in this section are for children from kindergarten through third grade. The directions have been kept simple, so the children can understand them easily after they've been read aloud. It is a good idea to play a game with a child or group of children before leaving them on their own.

These games involve only the concepts of addition and subtraction, and are arranged in order of increasing difficulty. The "Before" and "After" games are excellent for developing counting skills. Although none of the games involve decimal numbers, they can be used by simply introducing them as new numbers for the games.

Students can make up their own Mini-Mazes and give them to others to try. All the other games can be played with bigger numbers to substantially increase the level of difficulty.

Nim

For: Two players, one calculator.

Object: To try to get to 16.

How to play: Clear the calculator. Then, using only the digits 1, 2, and 3, take turns adding a digit to the display until somebody gets 16. Each player pushes a + after entering his or her number to see what the total is. The first player to push + and get to 16 wins — but if the total is over 16, the player has gone "bust," and loses.

Note: If the player who takes the second turn is very smart, he or she can always win the game! But only if the second player doesn't make any mistakes.

Sample Game

Jack lets Penny go first. They are playing with the keys 1, 2, 3, and +, with a goal of 16.

Penny	3 +	3
Jack	2 +	5
Penny	3 +	8
Jack	2 +	10
Penny	2 +	12

(Jack realizes he's been trapped! In resignation, he goes on.)

Jack	1 +	13
Penny	3 +	16

Penny wins. She knew after she got to 12 that she'd win. And she could have known even earlier.

Variations

Easier: Play to 21 or just to 11.

Harder: Play with the keys 1, 2, 3, 4, 5, 6, and the +. It changes the strategy quite a bit.

If you use the keys 1 through 9 and +, it changes the game still another way. This is easier than using the keys 1 through 6.

For two really experienced players, let the first player choose the goal number (it has to be below 70) and then let the second player choose the largest digit that can be used. For example, if the first player chooses 49, the second player might say the legal keys are 1, 2, 3, 4, 5, 6, and 7, and +.

Home Sweet Home

For: Two players and two calculators.

Needs: 2 markers (like a paper clip and a key) and 15 pennies or small pieces of paper to cover up the numbers.

Object: To get the marker home.

How to play: Using the trail shown on the facing page, one player puts his marker in the forest marked "1," and keys a 1 on his calculator. The other player puts his marker on 50, and enters 50 in his calculator.

The player on 1 then picks any number in the table and adds it on his calculator. With a penny or a piece of paper he covers the number he picked from the table.

The second player now chooses any uncovered number in the table, and subtracts it from the number in his calculator.

Players keep taking turns adding or subtracting numbers until one player gets home, or until all the numbers are covered. Players can add or subtract the number they select, no matter which forest they started from. If all the numbers get covered before anyone reaches home, the player closest to home wins.

Any player who goes off the path gets eaten up by the big bad wolf. (So make sure that you don't get a number that isn't on the path.)

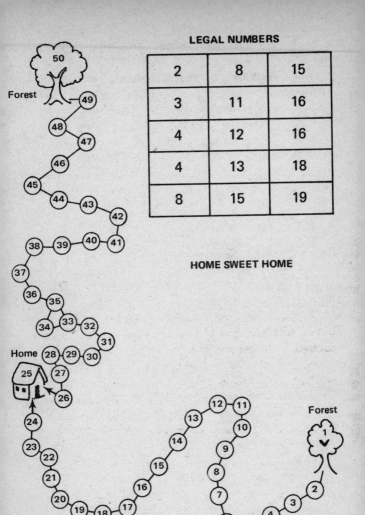

LEGAL NUMBERS

2	8	15
3	11	16
4	12	16
4	13	18
8	15	19

HOME SWEET HOME

Sample Game

Andy starts at 1, David at 50. Here is a short record of their game.

Andy   David

1 + 2 = 3   50 − 15 = 35

+ 19 = 22

(David sees that if Andy gets a 3, he'll be home, so David uses up the 3.)

                                   − 3 = 32

+ 8 = 30   − 11 = 21

(Andy sees that David is only 4 away from 25, so Andy takes one of the fours.)

− 4 = 26

(But there are two 4's on the chart, so David has one left to use.)

                                   + 4 = 25

Since David got to 25 first, he wins.

Note: Be sure you remember to cover each legal number after it has been used, so that it isn't used twice.

Variation

For a change, you can write in numbers from 1 to 20 and use them as your own table of legal numbers.

LEGAL NUMBERS

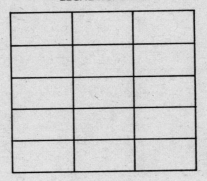

(make up your own)

Twenty Questions

For: Two or more players, one calculator.

Object: For the players to guess the number that one of them has written down.

How to play: One player is the "boss." The boss writes down a number from 1 to 100 on a piece of paper. He hides the paper so nobody else can see it.

The other players try to guess the number the boss wrote down. Each time a player makes a guess, the boss puts the secret number in the calculator and subtracts the guess. If the answer shows a minus sign then he answers, "Nope, your guess was too high." If the answer is not zero and doesn't have a minus sign, then the boss says, "No, your guess was too low." If the answer is zero, then the player has guessed the secret number, and the boss says, "You win."

The player who guesses the secret number gets to be the boss for the next game.

Sample Game

Jamie writes down the number 39 so the others can't see it. Then they take turns guessing his number.

Matt: 60   Jamie keys in 39 – 60 =, and gets –21. Since the answer has a – sign, he says, "Too high."

Sherrie: 30   Jamie keys 39 – 30 =, and gets 9. Since the answer doesn't have a – sign, he says, "Too low."

Rob: 40   Jamie keys 39 – 40 =, gets – 1. He says, "Too high."

Matt: 35   Jamie keys 39 – 35 =, gets 4.
                 He says, "Too low."

Sherrie: 38   Jamie keys 39 – 38 =, gets 1.
                 He says, "Too low," but he can't hide his
                 smile.

Rob, knowing he's got to be right, says, "39." Jamie says, "You're right," and pretends to throw the calculator down but gives it to Rob, who gets to name the next magic number.

Variations

Easier: Name a number that is smaller than 50. For very little kids, name a number that is smaller than 20. Or give hints, by telling whether the guess is way too small, or a lot too big. Or, at the beginning, say, "It has a 2 in it."

Harder: Start with a number that has four digits, like 3972. (The only change is that you have to say how many digits it has.)

After

For: Two or more young players, 1 calculator.

Object: To guess what number comes after the number on the display.

How to play: First, check to make sure the calculator has an addition constant (most small, inexpensive ones do). Key in 5 + = = = =. If the calculator adds 5 every time you push =, then it is fine for this game.

To start the game, clear the calculator. It is not cleared again until the end of the game. Then put in 1 + = = =. The calculator should count: 1, 2, 3. Now it is ready for the game.

One of the players keys in a number—let's say 23. The other players try to guess what number comes after 23. When everyone has made a guess, push =. The number after 23 will show on the display! See who guessed right.

Then another player can key in another number, and everybody guesses what comes after it.

Remember: Don't push C or CE (either of the Clear keys) between plays. It will make the calculator forget what number comes after the display.

Sample Game

Erin puts 1 + = = = in the calculator, just to make sure it is counting today.

Then Erin keys in 15, and asks Anna and Toby, "What comes after 15?"

Toby guesses it would be 25.

Anna thinks it is 16.

Erin pushes =, and the calculator shows 16, so Anna is right!

Without pushing another key, Erin gives the calculator to Anna, who puts in 27, then asks the others what they think comes after it.

Variations

Easier: Start with one-digit numbers like 5 or 8. Or you can key in a number, push = several times, then see if the child can say the next number.

Harder: Key in 10 + = instead of 1 + = at the beginning of the game. This will set the calculator counting in tens, rather than ones.

Before

For: Children who are good at "After." Requires one calculator.

Object: To guess what number comes before the number on the display.

How to play: Clear the calculator at the beginning of the game. Don't clear it again during the play.

One player keys in 10 - 1 = = = =. (The calculator should count backwards from 10. Otherwise, it isn't suited for this game.)

Without clearing the calculator, a player keys in a number such as 45. The other players try to guess what comes before 45. After everyone has made a guess, the player who put in 45 presses the = key. The number before 45 will show on the display.

The player who got it right goes next and keys in another number for everyone to guess the number before.

Remember: Don't clear the calculator between rounds.

Sample Game

Suzie, who wants to be a teacher when she grows up, challenges Greg and Randee to a game of "Before."

Greg keys in 10 - 1 = = =. Then, without pushing Clear, he hands the calculator to Suzie.

Suzie keys in 81, then asks the others, "What comes before 81?"

Greg answers, "80."

Randee thinks for a moment and guesses, "79."

Suzie pushes =, and 80 shows on the display.

"That's very good, Greg," says Suzie.

Greg shrugs. When he grows up, he wants to be David Brinkley. But right now he's busy with the calculator, and without clearing it he keys in his number.

Variations

Easier: Again, use one-digit numbers, such as 3 or 9.

Harder: Start off with 10 - = or with 2 - =. These make the game, "What comes 10 before the number?" or "What comes 2 before the number?" If your children are very bright or are in sixth grade, try starting with decimals— "What comes a tenth before the number," and start with .1 - =.

Wipeout

For: One or two players and a calculator.

Object: To wipe a single digit out of the display by subtracting only one number.

How to play: The player puts a patterned number in the calculator—for example: 12 345.987. Then the player tries to subtract a single number that will wipe out one digit without changing any of the others.

Note: Try to make up a number that is easy to remember so that you can see easily whether you've changed anything but the digit you wanted to wipe out. Numbers like 2468135 or 1.2345 or 54321.987 are good numbers, because if anything gets out of order, it's easy to spot. Numbers that are *not* good are 1323.4353 or 93857294, because in the first case there are too many of the same digit, and in the second number there is no pattern.

Sample Game

Janine keyed 12 345.678 into the calculator, then asked Joe to wipe out the 2. Joe thought for a minute, then keyed in − 2000 =. The calculator now read 10 345.678. Joe had wiped out the 2 without changing another digit.

Some easy wipeouts

Subtract a number (not a digit) to solve these.

Wipe the 4 out of 76 543 210

Wipe the 3 out of 13 245 768

Wipe the 9 out of 98 765 432

Some harder wipeouts

Wipe the 7 out of 34.567 891

Wipe the 1 out of 12 345.678

Knock the 6 out of 50 607 080

For supersurfers

Clean the 8 out of 2.468 135 7

Erase the 1 from 8.765 432 1

Wipe the 6 out of 3.040 506

Eliminate 1 from 3.000 001

Clear *all* the 5's from 1.525 354 5

A-Maze-in-Museum

For: One player and a calculator.

Object: To get the most points on your calculator as you go through the museum.

How to play: On the opposite page is a plan of a museum open to anyone with a pencil. The visitor starts with his pencil at the top, and goes down through the passages in the museum until he comes out the other side. Every time he goes through a passage he adds the number shown to his display. Once the visitor has been in a room, he can't go back to the same room again.

See how you can go through the museum with the most points on your calculator when you come out the back exit.

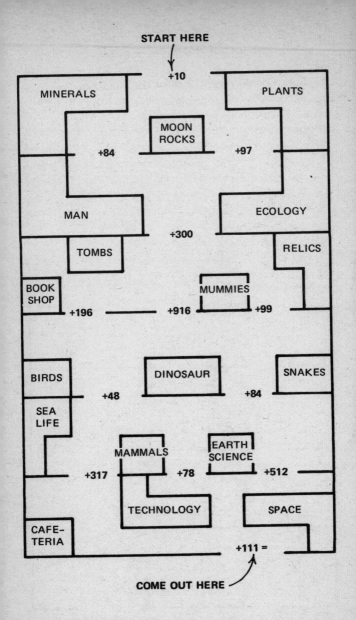

START HERE
+10

MINERALS

PLANTS

MOON ROCKS

+84   +97

MAN   ECOLOGY

+300

TOMBS   RELICS

BOOK SHOP   MUMMIES

+196   +916   +99

BIRDS   DINOSAUR   SNAKES

+48   +84

SEA LIFE

MAMMALS   EARTH SCIENCE

+317   +78   +512

TECHNOLOGY   SPACE

CAFE-TERIA

+111 =

COME OUT HERE

Write your own numbers beside the doors of this building. What is the biggest number you can get going through the building you made? Give your maze to somebody else, and see if they can get as big a number.

START HERE

COME OUT HERE

PATTERN PLAY

The diversions in this section are not games—they are just interesting calculator patterns that you might enjoy showing someone else. None of them are very complicated, yet the results are unexpected.

Key in the first number in each set as a constant multiplier. Then follow the keystrokes, writing down only the *last digit* in the display after each time you push the = key. Don't push Clear until the entire section is done.

8 x =   6 x =

    1 = = = = =   1 = = = = = =
      8 4 2 6 8   _ _ _ _ _ _

    2 = = = = = =   2 = = = = = =
      6 8 _ _ _ _   _ _ _ _ _ _

    3 = = = = =   3 = = = = = =
      _ _ _ _ _   _ _ _ _ _ _

    4 = = = = =   4 = = = = = =
      _ _ _ _ _   _ _ _ _ _ _

    5 = = = = =   5 = = = = = =
      _ _ _ _ _   _ _ _ _ _ _

    6 = = = = =   6 = = = = = =
      _ _ _ _ _   _ _ _ _ _ _

Continue each pattern through 9.

You can try the same sequence with other constants—and they all have regular patterns. The most regular are 5 and 0, of course, but the others are regular in their own ways.

The Alternator

Write down the number that is on your display after each step.

$7 - 77$ = _____

$+ 777$ = _____

$- 7\,777$ = _____

$+ 77\,777$ = _____

$- 777\,777$ = _____

$+ 7\,777\,777$ = _____

Try this one:

$.3 - .33$ = _____

$+ .333$ = _____

$- .333\,3$ = _____

$+ .333\,33$ = _____

$- .333\,333$ = _____

$+ .333\,333\,3$ = _____

These patterns will work with any digits. Make up a few of your own. The only thing to remember is to alternate subtracting with adding. (See formula on page 127.)

These patterns are a little different from the ones on the previous page. If you can figure them out, you'll be able to make up all sorts of alternators of your own. Again, write down the answer after each step.

$$5 - 555 \qquad = \rule{3cm}{0.4pt}$$

$$+ \; 55\,555 \qquad = \rule{3cm}{0.4pt}$$

$$- \; 5\,555\,555 \quad = \rule{3cm}{0.4pt}$$

$$.7 - .777 \qquad = \rule{3cm}{0.4pt}$$

$$+ \; .777\,77 \qquad = \rule{3cm}{0.4pt}$$

$$- \; .777\,777\,7 \; = \rule{3cm}{0.4pt}$$

Try this:

$$17 - 187 \qquad = \rule{3cm}{0.4pt}$$

$$+ \; 1\,887 \qquad = \rule{3cm}{0.4pt}$$

$$- \; 18\,887 \qquad = \rule{3cm}{0.4pt}$$

$$+ \; 188\,887 \qquad = \rule{3cm}{0.4pt}$$

$$- \; 1\,888\,887 \qquad = \rule{3cm}{0.4pt}$$

$$+ \; 18\,888\,887 \qquad = \rule{3cm}{0.4pt}$$

Division Diversion

This pattern play depends on finding the reciprocal of the number in your display. On most calculators, keying ÷ = = will give you the reciprocal of the number in the display. For example, 25 ÷ = = gives 0.04. On some calculators, 25 ÷ = gives 0.04. And on others, pressing the 1/x key gives the reciprocal.

Notice that the reciprocal of a two-digit number like 25 has two leading zeros in it—the zero before the decimal point, and the one before the 4. Find the reciprocals of the following numbers, and notice the pattern that occurs.

Three digits	Find the reciprocal	Leading zeros in the answer
924	÷ = =	_____
318	÷ = =	_____
106	÷ = =	_____
799	÷ = =	_____
Seven digits		
1 472 397	÷ = =	_____
9 371 397	÷ = =	_____
Two digits		
99	÷ = =	_____
13	÷ = =	_____

Five digits	Number of leading zeros in answer
38 141	_____
96 823	_____
11 048	_____
64 399	_____

One digit

7	_____
9	_____
4	_____
1	_____
6	_____

Try eight digits

84 204 633	_____
12 114 001	_____
64 846 732	_____

If your calculator doesn't show you the real answer, to the question involving eight digits, can you guess what the answer is? Try it on a calculator that has exponential notation and see if your guess is right.

Rotary Power

The only mathematics to remember in showing this trick to somebody is to press the + key. The result will never fail to amaze the person you try it out on.

Ask the person to press any three digit keys, except zero, then press the + key. In our example, Shirley pressed 186 +.

Now, turn the calculator clockwise 90°, so that it is at right angles to the way it was originally. Ask the person to push the digit keys now in the positions the original keys were. With the calculator turned, the 3 key is where the 1 used to be, the 4 is where the 8 used to be, and the 8 is where the 6 used to be. So Shirley keyed 348 +.

Turn the calculator again so it is upside down. Again, press the keys that are in the places the original keys were. In the drawing, notice that the digit 9 is where 1 used to be, 2 is where the 8 was, and 4 is where the 6 key was. So Shirley pressed 924 +.

Finally, turn the calculator clockwise 90° more. Again press the keys that are where the original keys were. This time Shirley pressed 762, since they are now where the 1, 8, and 6 keys were when the calculator was right side up.

Now push =. No matter what three digits the person started with originally, the answer will be the same as Shirley got: 2220.

Try the trick with four or five digits once you are good at remembering where the original digits were. You'll find that your answers follow the pattern—they just have more 2's in them.

SOLUTIONS

Page 25: **Hinkey Pinkey**

fat fowl = OBESE GEESE
pig puddle = HOG BOG
large jam-session = BIG GIG
bull's greeting = BELLO HELLO
company owners' liabilities = BOSSES LOSSES
Elizabeth I's supporters said, "BLESS BESS."
catch a queen = SEIZE BEES

Page 60: **unQuotable Quotes**

Rude pot-smokers are HIGH HEELS.
Caspar answers with "BOOO HOOO?"
HELLS BELLS would tell of the Devil's marriage.
Br'er Fox always told Br'er Rabbit to "LIE LO."

Page 63: **The Maze**

The highest score through the maze is 44.731 247,
achieved by following the segments: $+ 2 \div .9 \times 2.3 \times 1.95 \div .8 - .5 \times 2.7 - .8 \times 1.2 - 2 \div .8$.
The lowest possible score can be traced as follows:
$+ 3 \times .85 - 2 - .04 \div 1.8 \times .65 - .8 \div .37 - 2 \div .8$,
which comes to $- 4.580\ 518$.

Page 65: **Solitaire**

To get to 27 in ten strokes: $4 + 4 + 4 \div 4 \times = =$.
Or on some calculators: $4 + = = \div 4 = \times = =$.
On a Rockwell 18R, an *eight*-stroke solution is possible: $4 + + \div = \times = =$.

Page 65: **Solitaire** Group I

From 91 to 21:   91 ÷ 7 + 4 = =.
From 3 to 32:   3 x 9 + 5 =.
From 4 to 19:   4 x = + 3 =.
From 13 to 58:   13 ÷ = + 5 7 =.
From 72 to 20:   72 ÷ 8 + = + 2 =.
From 64 to 48:   64 – 61 x 16 =.

Page 66: **Solitaire** Group II

From 9 to 14:   Begin with 9, they key 8 ÷ 7 =.
From 12 to 50:   Begin with 12, then key .5 x 4 =.
From 10 to 73:   Begin with 10, then key ÷ = + 7 x =
                                 + 9 =.
From 31 to 56:   Begin with 31, then key x . = 8 x 7 =.

Solitaire Group III

From 2 to 77:   Begin with 2, then key – 5 = x = = =
                                 – 4 =.
From 4 to 62:   Begin with 4, then key 7 7 ÷ 9 + 9 =.
From 1 to 256:   Begin with 1, then key 9 – 3 ÷ = =
                                 ÷ = = =.
From 2 to 27:   Begin with 2, then key ÷ 5 + 5 x 5 =.
From 8 to 199:   Begin with 8, then key 7 – 7 3 = x =
                                 + 3 =.
From 4 to 100:   Begin with 4, then key ÷ = = + 6 x 1
                                 6 =.

Page 67: **Solitaire** Group IV

To get to 110:   33 ÷ .3 =.
To get to 424:   8 ÷ = = ÷ = = = = – 8 8 =.
To get to 49:   8 ÷ = – 8 x =.
To get to 100:   7 7 – 7 ÷ . 7 =.
To get to 936:   6 + = = + 8 x 6 = =.

(On some calculators: x 6 before the final =.)

The key to the labyrinth is a small part of the final few segments of the puzzle.

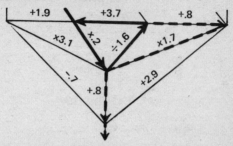

No matter what score you have when you get to the triangle if you keep going around it in the direction x .2 ÷ 1.6 + 3.7, after a number of rounds 4.228 571 4 will come up every time after you add the 3.7. Go part of the way around again, x .2, ÷ 1.6 = .528 571 4, then cut off at + .8 x 1.7 + .8 = and your answer will be 3.058 571 3. This is the lowest you can score going through the labyrinth.

Page 80: Doubles

The scoring doesn't really reflect the chance of getting a triple or a quad accurately. The chances of getting a double are 7 x 1/10, or 7/10. The chances of getting a triple are 6 x 1/10 x 1/10, or 6/100. Your chances of getting a triple are less than 1/10 as good as your chances of getting a double. The chances of having a quad come into view are really slim—5 x 1/10 x 1/10 x 1/10, or 5/1000. The odds of getting a quad are less than a hundredth the chances of getting a double, yet the score is only four times greater. How come? Unfortunately, if the scoring had been based on these probabilities, a single lucky hit would have meant that nobody else would have had a chance.

The probability of each hand was computed according to the probabilities below. You'll notice that the chances of a nothing hand—that is, not even a pair—is actually lower than the chance that the hand will contain a pair. But because the non-counting hand is seen as uninteresting in real poker games, we'll leave it out of the priorities chart.

Five of a kind	$(.1)^5 (10)$	.00010
Flush (odd or even)	$(.1)^5 (120)$	.00120
Four of a kind	$(.1)^5 (45) (2) (5)$	.00450
Straight	$(1.)^5 (7) (120)$	.00840
Full house	$(.1)^5 (45) (2) (10)$	.00900
Three of a kind	$(.1)^5 (120) (3) (10) (2)$	.07200
Two pair	$(.1)^5 (120) (3) (10) (3)$	.108
One pair	$(.1)^5 (210) (4) (10) (3) (2)$	.504
All others		.2916

(This chart was prepared with the assistance of Tom Knapp.)

Page 118: **The Alternator**

The general form of the pattern is this:

$$n - 11(n) + 111(n) - 1\,111(n) + 11\,111(n) \ldots$$

where n is any one-digit number, or where n is any two-digit number the sum of whose digits is not greater than 10. The most interesting case is where the sum of the digits is exactly 10, because of the dissimilarity of the numbers added and subtracted from the original number, and from the result.